THE
AMERICAN CATHOLIC
PEOPLE

THE AMERICAN CATHOLIC PEOPLE:

Their Beliefs, Practices, and Values

George Gallup, Jr., and Jim Castelli

Doubleday & Company, Inc., Garden City, New York, 1987

Library of Congress Cataloging-in-Publication Data

Gallup, George, 1930–
The American Catholic people.

Includes index.
1. Catholics—United States. 2. Catholic Church—
United States—History—20th century. 3. United States
—Church history—20th century. I. Castelli, Jim.
II. Title.
BX1406.2.G35 1987   282'.0973   86-16576
ISBN 0-385-23122-9

CONTENTS

FOREWORD

The American Catholic People: Their Beliefs, Practices, and Values is an effort to develop a fleshed-out portrait of American Catholics by mining the considerable amount of data generated by the Gallup Organization. We have tried to show what American Catholics look like, how they think, and how they behave; we have examined their demographics, their religious beliefs and practices, and their opinions on a broad range of social and political issues. In portraying American Catholics, we have also painted a picture of the varieties of American Protestantism, and that, too, will be useful.

But first a word about this study's methodology and limits. Our approach is basically archaeological—it took a lot of digging. First, we examined more than two decades of Gallup polls, from 1965 to early 1986. Second, we analyzed data from a number of special Gallup studies conducted for various religious organizations. We would particularly like to cite the following:

▪ *U.S. Catholics and the Catholic Press,* conducted for the Catholic Press Association, 1978.

▪ *A Gallup Study of Religious and Social Attitudes of Hispanic-Americans,* conducted for *Our Sunday Visitor,* 1978.

▪ *The Unchurched American,* conducted for a coalition of religious denominations and organizations, 1978.

▪ *Women in Ministry,* 1978.

▪ *Evangelical Christianity in the United States,* conducted for *Christianity Today,* 1979.

▪ *Jesus Christ in the Lives of Americans Today,* conducted for the Robert H. Schuller Ministries, 1982.

▪ *The Spiritual Climate in America Today,* conducted for the Christian Broadcasting Network, 1983.

▪ *24 Hours in the Religious and Spiritual Life of America,* conducted for the Christian Broadcasting Network, 1984.

▪ *How Can Christian Liberals and Conservatives Be Brought Together?,* conducted for the Robert H. Schuller Ministries, 1984.

▪ *Religion and Television,* conducted for the Ad Hoc Committee on Electronic Church Research, 1984.

▪ *Attitudes of Unchurched Americans Toward the Roman Catholic Church,* conducted for the National Catholic Evangelization Association, 1985.

▪ *17th Annual Survey of the Public's Attitudes Toward the Public Schools,* conducted for Phi Delta Kappa, Inc., 1985.

▪ *Trends in Catholic Lay Attitudes Since Vatican II on Church Life and Leadership,* Report #5, *Study of Future Church Leadership,* conducted for Dean R. Hoge, Department of Sociology, Catholic University of America, 1986.

Several factors must be kept in mind in reading this book:

1. All our data are based on samples of self-defined Catholics aged eighteen and over, that is, people who identify themselves as Catholic when asked their religion. We know that about 20 percent of this group say they are not church members, so findings for this group would be different from those of a sample of Catholics with actual parish ties. The Protestant sample we are working with also contains about 20 percent who are not church members, so we are comparing like groups of Catholics and Protestants. But self-identification is a significant process and one very legitimate definition of "Catholic."

2. In most of these surveys, the number of Catholics is between four hundred and five hundred and the number of Protestants a little more than eight hundred. Here is the margin of error for standard samples closest to those figures:

SIZE OF SAMPLE

	750	400
PERCENTAGES NEAR 10	3	4
PERCENTAGES NEAR 20	4	5
PERCENTAGES NEAR 30	4	6
PERCENTAGES NEAR 40	4	6
PERCENTAGES NEAR 50	4	6
PERCENTAGES NEAR 60	4	6

	750	*400*
PERCENTAGES NEAR 70	4	6
PERCENTAGES NEAR 80	4	5
PERCENTAGES NEAR 90	3	4

Because of the margin of error in samples this size, we have tried to emphasize trends and patterns and not place too much emphasis on any single response. For example, a small difference between Catholics and Protestants on one question may not be conclusive; but if that same difference appears when the same question is asked several times over a period of years, we can reach a conclusion with more confidence. Similarly, if several differently worded questions reveal the same pattern, we can have greater confidence in interpreting that pattern.

3. In some particularly interesting areas, we have only one set of data from several years back; in general, old data are better than no data. But if the material involves some core philosophical values, which are not usually subject to sudden change, it will be significantly more valuable than, for example, looking back to see who Catholics favored in the presidential primaries in April 1976.

4. While we were able to make comparisons between Catholics and Protestants and at times between Catholics and Evangelicals or members of specific Protestant denominations, we did not have large enough samples to include Jews in the comparisons. Such a comparison would, no doubt, be fascinating, but it was simply impossible.

5. Finally, with the exception of some data on Hispanic Catholics, we do not have breakdowns of Catholics by ethnic backgrounds. We are confident that ethnic breakdowns would reveal differences as fascinating as those between different Protestant denominations, but that, too, was impossible.

Even with these limitations, however, we believe that we have made some real discoveries, which we hope will be the subject of discussion within the Church, the social science community, and the nation at large. Some of our findings call for further research, some for further reflection.

I. PROFILE

The election of John Fitzgerald Kennedy as the first Catholic President of the United States, in 1960, was a turning point in American history: With that election, American Catholics came of age politically. The only previous Catholic presidential candidate, New York Governor Alfred E. Smith, who won the 1928 Democratic nomination, won only eighty-seven electoral votes in a landslide loss to Herbert Hoover following a campaign often dominated by anti-Catholicism. Even though Roman Catholics have made up the largest single religious denomination in the country since 1850, for more than a century after that they remained a self-conscious and suspect minority: Their religious allegiance to the Pope, the Bishop of Rome, was seen by some as political allegiance to a foreign power. There were three major waves of anti-Catholicism between the early-nineteenth and early-twentieth centuries; "Kathlics" ranked with "Kikes" and "Koons" as targets of the Ku Klux Klan. Many Catholics responded to the distrust of some other Americans by becoming superpatriotic: They were often the last group to question U.S. foreign policy.

Shortly after Kennedy's election, another Catholic named John made history when Pope John XXIII called the Second Vatican Council to, in his words, "open a window on the world." With the Council, the dominant fact in twentieth-century Catholicism, Catholics—and American Catholics in particular—came of age religiously. The Council offered strong support for religious freedom and for cooperation with other Christians, non-Christians, and nonbelievers, and it committed the Church to involvement on behalf of social justice. It also launched a series of internal church reforms, including a wider role for the laity and liturgical changes such as allowing the celebration of the Mass in the vernacular, local languages instead of in Latin.

Throughout this period, American Catholics, thanks in part to the

G.I. Bill, were moving up in income and education and a whole generation was growing up without a sense of being second-class citizens.
Today American Catholics no longer worry about being accepted—they
worry about how to lead. In the quarter century since Kennedy's election, American Catholics have developed a stunning momentum—eco-
nomically, socially, politically, spiritually—that ensures that they will
have a profound impact on the shape of American society a quarter
century from now. Their influence also extends beyond our shores:
American Catholics often set the pace for Catholics in other countries.
The Vatican's nuncio, or representative, to the United States, Archbishop Pio Laghi, says, "When it's raining in the United States, it's
cloudy overseas."

At one level, American Catholics are influential because of their
numbers. The relative growth of the Catholic population in the United
States is a remarkable story. In 1947, 20 percent of adults surveyed said
their religious preference was Catholic; today that figure is 28 percent.
Thus, the percentage of Americans who call themselves Catholic has
grown by almost one half in forty years. But, in 1947, 69 percent of
Americans called themselves Protestant—outnumbering Catholics by a
ratio of more than three to one. Today, however, 58 percent of Americans call themselves Protestant, reducing the Protestant/Catholic ratio
to 2:1. There are three major reasons for this shift: a higher birth rate
among Catholics during this period, the influx of largely Catholic Hispanic immigrants, and a decline in membership in mainline Protestant
churches, particularly among Methodists, Presbyterians, and Episcopalians.

If we were to make a straight-line projection on the basis of this
trend, we could conclude that somewhere in the middle of the next
century, Catholics would vie with Protestants as the dominant religion
in America. Further support for such a conclusion seems warranted
when we examine the religious affiliation pattern among young adults
and teenagers—as many as one third of America's teenagers give their
religious preference as Catholic, a higher percentage than in the adult
population.

In addition to this remarkable growth, another dramatic shift has
taken place in recent decades: For the first time in the history of the
nation, the proportion of Catholics in "upscale" groups (upper income
and education levels) matches the proportion of Protestants. In addition, a higher percentage of Catholics are currently found in the college,
than in the general, population, suggesting that Catholics are poised for
even further gains in education and income.

Catholics have become increasingly more visible in the public eye. For example, Chrysler chairman Lee Iacocca has become a modern folk hero, ranking high on the list of most-admired men. Catholics also seem to have a particular vocation to politics. In 1962 there were 99 Catholics in Congress; in 1984 there were 142. Many of the major political figures of recent years have been Catholic: Representative Peter Rodino and Judge John Sirica, heroes of the Watergate era; Senator Edward Kennedy; former House Speaker Tip O'Neill; vice-presidential candidate Geraldine Ferraro; New York governor Mario Cuomo.

Catholic religious leadership has also become more visible. Pope John Paul II, with his strong personality and commitment to human rights, is highly popular with many Americans, not just Catholics. The U.S. bishops moved to the forefront of the antinuclear movement with their 1983 pastoral letter, *The Challenge of Peace*, and with their 1986 pastoral letter on economic justice.

Who are today's American Catholic people? One of the most striking things about them is their youth: Twenty-nine percent are under thirty, 36 percent are between thirty and forty-nine, and 35 percent are over fifty. In contrast, 24 percent of Protestants are under thirty and 41 percent are over fifty. The difference is even more pronounced when we compare Catholics to mainline Protestant denominations. Only 18 percent of Methodists, Presbyterians, and Episcopalians are under thirty; 46 percent of Episcopalians and 48 percent of Methodists and Presbyterians are over fifty. The higher birth rate among Catholics in the "Baby Boom" generation and among Hispanic Catholics accounts for a large part of this difference. But part of the explanation is the difficulty mainline Protestant denominations have had in retaining young people.

American Catholics have long been an immigrant people, and that tradition is continuing today. One in five Catholics now belong to minority groups. Hispanics now make up 16 percent of American Catholics—more than eleven million people. Three percent of Catholics—two million people—are black. Another 3 percent of Catholics describe themselves as "nonwhite"; since very few Hispanics identify themselves as "nonwhite," this suggests that the influx of Catholic immigrants from Southeast Asia is starting to show up in national surveys. Among Protestants, 14 percent are black and 2 percent are Hispanic. This means that while the percentage of blacks among Protestants is five times that among Catholics, a higher percentage of Catholics overall come from minority groups.

Since at least the mid-1960s, Catholics have equaled Protestants in education and income levels. But, as is true in a number of cases, the overall figures for Protestants mask significant differences between denominations. When we compare Catholics with individual denominations, we find them still ranking behind Presbyterians and Episcopalians, about on a par with Lutherans and Methodists, and well ahead of Baptists on education and income scales. Of course, even these comparisons mask the impact of lower-income minorities on the overall Catholic figures: Considerably more Catholics than Methodists, Lutherans, Presbyterians, and Episcopalians belong to minority groups. This suggests that non-Hispanic white Catholics rank slightly ahead of Lutherans and Methodists in income levels. The percentage of Catholics with incomes above $40,000 a year ranks behind the percentage of Presbyterians and Episcopalians and is about the same as Methodists and Lutherans. Of course, the relative size of the populations—Catholics make up 28 percent of the population, and Presbyterians and Episcopalians 2 percent each—means that the new Catholic affluence will have a greater impact on the country at large.

	$40,000 and above	$30,000–39,999
EPISCOPALIAN	29	11
PRESBYTERIAN	23	14
CATHOLIC	17	13
LUTHERAN	16	15
METHODIST	16	11
PROTESTANT	14	11
SOUTHERN BAPTIST	11	10
BAPTIST	9	9

A similar pattern can be found in employment. The proportion of Catholics, Methodists, and Lutherans in business and the professions is virtually identical, running ahead of Baptists and behind Presbyterians and Episcopalians.

	Business/ Professional	Clerical/ Sales	Manual	Non-labor Force
EPISCOPALIAN	50	6	20	21
PRESBYTERIAN	42	8	21	23
LUTHERAN	31	7	33	19

	Business/ Professional	Clerical/ Sales	Manual	Non-labor Force
CATHOLIC	30	7	39	17
METHODIST	30	6	31	25
PROTESTANT	27	7	37	21
SOUTHERN BAPTIST	22	7	42	22
BAPTIST	20	7	44	21

Following a national trend, the percentage of Catholics with a college background has more than doubled in the past twenty years. These figures show the percentage of college graduates and those with some college background by denomination for 1984:

	College Graduate	College Incomplete
EPISCOPALIAN	34	29
PRESBYTERIAN	30	29
LUTHERAN	19	25
METHODIST	19	23
CATHOLIC	17	24
PROTESTANT	17	22
SOUTHERN BAPTIST	10	20
BAPTIST	9	19

Catholics remain an urban people, although one in four live in rural areas. Even so, a higher percentage of Catholics (39 percent) than of any other major denomination live in center cities, and 35 percent live in suburbs:

	Center City	Suburbs	Rural
CATHOLIC	39	35	26
BAPTIST	32	17	51
EPISCOPALIAN	30	38	32
PROTESTANT	26	23	51
PRESBYTERIAN	24	34	42
SOUTHERN BAPTIST	24	17	59
LUTHERAN	22	28	50
METHODIST	20	21	59

Catholics also remain concentrated in the Northeast and the Midwest, although there has been a substantial shift toward the Sun Belt. In 1966, only 9 percent of Catholics lived in the South and 13 percent in the West; in 1984, 17 percent lived in the South and 18 percent in the West. In other words, the percentage of Catholics in the Northeast and the Midwest decreased from 78 to 65 percent. Catholics make up 44 percent of the population in the East, 26 percent in the Midwest, 16 percent in the South, and 26 percent in the West.

The makeup of American Catholics is changing in terms of family status. The percentage of Catholics who are married has dropped since 1976, while the percentage that are single, separated, or divorced has increased. In 1985, 8 percent of Catholics were divorced and 2 percent were separated; this does not count divorced and remarried Catholics. One Catholic teenager in four say that their natural parents have been divorced, the same rate found in the general population.

The percentage of Catholics currently separated or divorced doubled —from 5 to 10 percent—between 1976 and 1985. During the same period, the percentage of those currently married dropped from 69 to 62 percent, and the percentage never married rose from 19 to 22 percent.

Sixty-eight percent of American Catholics have had children: 15 percent have had one child, 19 percent have had two, 15 percent have had three, 8 percent have had four, 6 percent have had five, and 5 percent have had six or more.

Catholics have historically favored larger families than have other Americans, but by 1985 the difference in ideal family size between Catholics and Protestants had disappeared as Catholics became part of the mainstream, which considered two children the ideal family size. As recently as 1968, there was a substantial gap on the issue, with 50 percent of Catholics and 37 percent of Protestants saying that four or more children was the ideal family size. Even in January 1983, there was still a 6-point gap. But in February 1985, there was no statistical difference between the two groups: Only 9 percent of Catholics and 10 percent of Protestants chose large families (four or more children) as the ideal. This trend should not come as a surprise. Despite the Catholic Church's condemnation of artificial means of birth control, American Catholics have favored access to contraceptives and information about them in the same proportion as the rest of the population since the 1950s.

This trend could change, however; among teenagers, 18 percent of

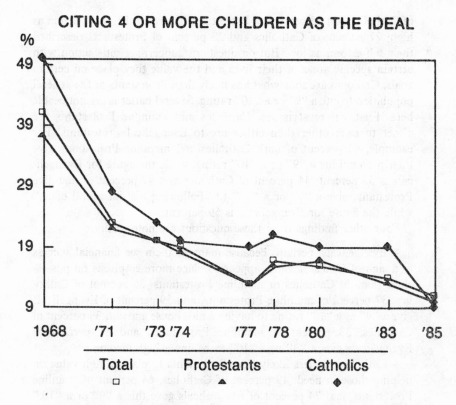

CITING 4 OR MORE CHILDREN AS THE IDEAL

%

49 —

39 —

29 —

19 —

9 —

1968   '71   '73 '74   '77 '78 '80   '83   '85

Total   Protestants   Catholics
  □   ▲   ◆

Catholics and 9 percent of Protestants cite four or more children as the ideal family size.

A profile of American Catholics would not be complete without a look at the self-perception of Catholics. For example, there is no difference between Catholics and Protestants in reported levels of satisfaction with the way things are going in their personal lives, with about eight in ten saying they are satisfied. Both groups are considerably less satisfied with the way things are going in the nation, although that dissatisfaction does not affect personal satisfaction, which has remained fairly constant as satisfaction with the state of the nation rose from two in ten in 1979 to five in ten in 1984. Catholics have consistently—though by only a few percentage points—been slightly more satisfied with the state of the nation.

Catholics rank slightly higher than Protestants or the general population in perception of their own level of self-esteem. Thirty-nine percent of Catholics and 35 percent of Protestants described their self-esteem as high; 27 percent of Catholics and 30 percent of Protestants described their self-esteem as low. But on questions concerning satisfaction with certain specific areas of their lives and the value they place on certain goals, Catholics are somewhat less likely than Protestants or the general population to cite a "9" or a "10" rating. Several patterns are noticeable here. First, on most issues, Catholics and mainline Protestants are closer to each other than either are to Evangelical Protestants. For example, 43 percent of both Catholics and mainline Protestants give their personal life a "9" or a "10" rating, while the figure for Evangelicals is 53 percent; 44 percent of Catholics and 47 percent of mainline Protestants give a "9" or a "10" to "Following a strict moral code," while the figure for Evangelicals is 59 percent.

Four other findings from these questions are noteworthy:

▪ Evangelicals, perhaps because many of them see financial success as a sign of God's blessing, appear to place more emphasis on possessions than do Catholics or mainline Protestants: 36 percent of Catholics, 37 percent of mainline Protestants, and 59 percent of Evangelicals give a "9" or a "10" rating to having a nice house and car; 39 percent of Catholics, 33 percent of mainline Protestants, and 51 percent of Evangelicals give a "9" or a "10" to having a high income.

▪ Catholics are less likely than Protestants to place a high value on helping those in need: 49 percent of Catholics, 64 percent of mainline Protestants, and 74 percent of Evangelicals gave this a "9" or a "10." One explanation for this difference may be that Protestants place a greater emphasis on individual, one-on-one charity.

▪ Eighty percent of Catholics, mainline Protestants, and Evangelicals gave the goal of good self-image and self-respect a "9" or a "10," matching the proportion for the general population. This seems to be an area of absolute national consensus—the American way places a high value on self-respect.

▪ Catholics were closer to Evangelicals than to mainline Protestants in their ranking of the importance of social recognition: 28 percent of Catholics, 27 percent of Evangelicals, and 19 percent of mainline Protestants gave this value a "9" or a "10." This slight difference may reflect the degree to which both Catholics and Evangelicals still feel they are "outsiders."

Finally, there is no difference between Catholics and Protestants in terms of their political self-perception: 33 percent of Catholics and 32 percent of Protestants describe themselves as left-of-center, 12 percent of Catholics and 10 percent of Protestants describe themselves as middle-of-the-road, and 55 percent of Catholics and 58 percent of Protestants describe themselves as right-of-center. But there is a significant difference in self-perception concerning values toward sex, morality, family life, and religion. With a "1" indicating the most conservative position and a "7" the most liberal, 60 percent of Protestants and only 47 percent of Catholics placed themselves at less than "4," the middle-of-the-road position; in contrast, 29 percent of Catholics and only 19 percent of Protestants placed themselves in the "5–7," or liberal, category.

CONCLUSION

All in all, in examining some basic facts about American Catholics, we find a generally young, well-educated, upbeat, and upscale group. Now we will take a closer look at their religious beliefs and practices and their social attitudes.

II. RELIGIOUS BELIEF

Do Catholics and Protestants have distinctly different religious beliefs, or do their views reflect their common Christianity? The answer is "Both." At one level, there is virtual agreement between Catholics and Protestants on basic beliefs about the nature of God and Jesus Christ. There are obvious differences related to church structure and tradition, such as Catholic belief in the papacy. But there are also other, deeper differences in religious belief that produce significantly different religious worldviews. Because behavior follows belief, those differing worldviews account for much of the difference in attitude and practice between American Catholics and American Protestants.

We have identified from surveys five basic ways in which the Catholic religious worldview differs from the Protestant worldview. The result of these differences is what might be called the "intensity factor."

1. The Catholic worldview is intellectual; it is more likely to reconcile reason and faith than the Protestant worldview, which sees a greater tension between the two and leans heavily toward reliance on faith.

2. The Catholic worldview is accepting; it takes a more understanding attitude toward sinners and toward those who hold different religious views.

3. The Catholic worldview is pragmatic and earthy; it is marked by an intense concern with this world and a much lower priority on the next.

4. The Catholic worldview is communal; it places a greater emphasis on social justice as a dimension of faith and a corresponding lower priority on personal piety.

5. The Catholic worldview is private; it views religion as an individual choice and does not actively seek the conversion of others.

These differences must be viewed in context. The deeper one examines religious belief and practice, the less accurate the umbrella label of "Protestant" appears. Denominational differences among Protestants are great; in particular, the differences between Evangelical and mainline Protestants are often immense. In fact, on a great many issues, mainline Protestants are closer to Catholics than they are to Evangelical Protestants.

Within this context, the overall pattern of the Catholic-Protestant differences that we see shows that Catholics are more liberal than Protestants in their religious beliefs. A variety of findings confirm this impression. The first involves a question asking people to place themselves on a scale of religious ideology, with "1" representing the most conservative position and "6" the most liberal. If we group "1" and "2" as conservative, "3" and "4" as moderate, and "5" and "6" as liberal, there is not much difference between Catholics and Protestants. But if we draw the line a little differently and count a "3" as leaning conservative and a "4" as leaning liberal, the picture shifts radically. In that case, we find 34 percent of Catholics leaning conservative and 49 percent leaning liberal; we then find 47 percent of Protestants leaning conservative and 40 percent leaning liberal.

RELIGIOUS VIEWS

	1	2	3	4	5	6
CATHOLIC	5	8	21	31	9	9
PROTESTANT	8	13	26	24	10	6

This pattern is confirmed when we compare Catholic self-assessments to those of members of other denominations; once again, we note that mainline Protestants occupy a middle ground between Catholics and Evangelicals:

	1	2	3	4	5	6
CATHOLIC	5	8	21	31	9	9
EVANGELICAL	15	23	22	17	7	4
BAPTIST	8	17	24	24	11	7
SOUTHERN BAPTIST	13	11	29	14	16	9
METHODIST	3	10	31	31	9	6

A review of trends involving responses to two key indicators of religious views indicates that while there has been a decline in expressed importance of religion and confidence in religion's ability to answer our problems, the decline has been greater among Catholics. In fact, there has been a significant shift: Catholics were more pious than Protestants in the 1950s, but are less so today. For example, in 1952, 83 percent of Catholics and 76 percent of Protestants said religion was "very important" to them; but, by 1984, the percentage of Catholics making this statement had dropped to 53 percent, lower than the 62 percent of Protestants saying religion was "very important" to them.

RELIGION "VERY IMPORTANT"

	Cath.	Prot.	Total	Bapt.	Meth.	Luth.	Psbt.
1952	83	76	75	84	74	70	72
1965	76	74	70	82	65	66	71
1978	51	60	52	—	—	—	—
1980	56	61	55	68	52	57	48
1983	56	62	56	69	56	55	55
1984	53	62	56	69	55	56	53

A similar pattern emerges in response to the question: "Do you believe that religion can answer all or most of today's problems, or that religion is largely old-fashioned and out of date?" In 1957, 83 percent of both Catholics and Protestants said religion could answer all or most of the day's problems. In 1985, the number of Protestants answering in the affirmative had fallen to 70 percent, while the response among Catholics had declined to only 52 percent.

A third trend indicates a Catholic/Protestant reversal since the 1950s. In 1957, 78 percent of Americans answered "Yes" to the question: "Do you think a person can be a good Christian if he doesn't go to church?" In 1978, the identical percentage answered "Yes" to the question: "Can a person be a good Christian or Jew without going to church or synagogue?" But, in 1957, Protestants (80 percent) were slightly more likely than Catholics (73 percent) to say "Yes." By 1978, however, Catholics (81 percent) were more likely than Protestants (75 percent) to say "Yes."

These three trends suggest that, in relation to one another, American Catholics are becoming more independent and turning outward, while American Protestants are turning inward as far as the church is con-

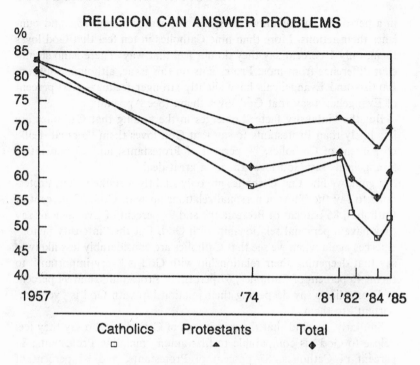

cerned. This conclusion would be supported by the general history of the two groups over that period. American Catholics, sparked by the Second Vatican Council, have indeed been turning outward, leaving the era of ghetto Catholicism behind and becoming more sure of themselves in both church and society. American Protestants, on the other hand, have gone through a more difficult time. Mainline Protestants have seen their sense of cultural dominance eroded and have undergone a kind of crisis of confidence. Evangelical Protestants have gone through a period of withdrawal from the culture, followed by a period of intense involvement in an effort to transform the culture. It is easy to see how this would translate into a greater erosion of outward concern about religion among Catholics than among Protestants.

The most basic agreements between Catholics and Protestants in the area of religious belief can be found in their beliefs about the existence and nature of God. Beliefs about God also illustrate the "intensity factor." For example, we begin with agreement: 98 percent of both groups believe in God or a universal spirit; seven in ten in both groups believe in a personal God or universal spirit who watches, rewards, and punishes their actions. More than nine Catholics in ten feel that God loves them; only 1 percent say they do not feel that way. There is no significant difference from most Protestants on this issue, although Southern Baptists and Evangelicals have slightly stronger feelings—100 percent of Evangelicals say that God loves them. (See Appendix.)

But the "intensity factor" emerges in the finding that Catholics are less likely than Protestants to say that God loves them "a great deal": 65 percent of Catholics, 79 percent of Protestants, and 92 percent of Evangelicals say God loves them "a great deal."

Again, we find that Catholics are only slightly less likely than Protestants to say they have a personal relationship with God: 82 percent of Catholics, 86 percent of Protestants, and 97 percent of Evangelicals say they have a personal relationship with God. But the "intensity factor" emerges again when we see that Catholics are considerably less likely to say that deepening their relationship with God is "very important" to them: 46 percent of Catholics, 67 percent of Protestants, and 94 percent of Evangelicals say deepening their relationship with God is "very important" to them.

Similarly, we find that the percentage of Catholics who say they feel "close to God" is comparable to that among mainline Protestants: 83 percent of Catholics, 87 percent of Protestants, and 95 percent of Evangelicals say they felt "close to God" in the past year.

But the "intensity factor" again emerges when we see that Catholics are less likely to answer "Yes" to the question: "Have you ever been aware of, or influenced by, a presence or a power—whether you call it God or not—which is different from your everyday life?" Thirty-seven percent of Catholics, 48 percent of Protestants, and 52 percent of Southern Baptists said they had felt such a presence. One reason for this difference may be that the more intense, overtly pious nature of Protestant belief makes Protestants more alert to this sort of experience—or more likely to describe experiences as God's presence.

If Catholics have a less personal relationship with God than do Protestants, they also have less fear of God—twice as many Baptists and Evangelicals as Catholics reported feeling afraid of God within the past year.

WITHIN THE LAST YEAR, FELT AFRAID OF GOD

	Yes	No
BAPTIST	26	69
EVANGELICAL	24	74
PROTESTANT	19	76
EPISCOPALIAN	17	79
METHODIST	14	80
LUTHERAN	13	81
CATHOLIC	11	85
PRESBYTERIAN	11	86

The lack of fear of God among Catholics may be related to their sense of what God expects. For example, a survey conducted for Dean Hoge at Catholic University found that 72 percent of Catholics agree that: "God doesn't really care how he is worshiped as long as he is worshiped"; only 20 percent disagreed. Just as Catholics are less likely than Protestants to report feeling afraid of God, they are less likely to report having felt guilty of sin during the past year:

GUILTY OF SIN

	Yes	No
EVANGELICAL	69	27
LUTHERAN	60	35
PRESBYTERIAN	60	39
PROTESTANT	58	37
BAPTIST	57	36
METHODIST	54	41
EPISCOPALIAN	53	43
CATHOLIC	50	45

While Catholics and Protestants are extremely close in their beliefs about God, they differ somewhat in their beliefs about the Devil. Here, too, we see the "intensity factor" at work. Three in four in both groups believe the Devil exists, but Catholics are more inclined to view the Devil as an impersonal force that influences people to do wrong, while Protestants are more inclined to view the Devil as a personal being who directs evil forces and influences people to do wrong. Here, too, the views of Catholics and mainline Protestants are closer to each other than either are to those of Baptists:

THE DEVIL

	Personal Being	Impersonal Force	Does not exist
SOUTHERN BAPTIST	53	38	6
BAPTIST	52	36	6
PROTESTANT	40	36	16
LUTHERAN	34	36	21
CATHOLIC	32	41	19
METHODIST	24	47	21

But Catholics seem a bit uncertain about the nature of evil and its relationship to God—only 51 percent believe that God will punish evil for all eternity, while 32 percent do not believe that statement and 17 percent are undecided.

The similarity between Catholic and Protestant beliefs about God extend to their beliefs about Jesus: 79 percent of Catholics and 75 percent of Protestants believe that Jesus was God; more than 70 percent in both groups have no doubts that Jesus was fully God and fully human. More than 80 percent in both groups believe that Jesus is alive in some fashion today—in Heaven, in the world, in people, in themselves. The only significant difference comes in beliefs about the Second Coming: 74 percent of Protestants and only 59 percent of Catholics believe that Jesus will return to earth. One reason for this difference may be the greater emphasis on the Second Coming found in Protestant—particularly Evangelical—churches.

But, in another example of the "intensity factor," Catholics are less likely to describe the belief that Jesus is fully God and fully human as "very important" to them: 58 percent of Catholics, 67 percent of Protestants, and 92 percent of Evangelicals say this belief is "very important." And while 58 percent of Catholics believe one cannot be a "true Christian" without believing in the divinity of Christ, 30 percent— double the figure for Protestants—believe that it is possible to be a true Christian without believing in the divinity of Christ.

There is more similarity between Catholics and Protestants in their views about what someone who is trying to be a follower of Jesus should do. About half of both groups cite obeying the Ten Commandments;

just under half of each say that a Christian must forgive those who have wronged him; about one third say a Christian must put others' needs before his own. There were several interesting differences in this area. One clearly reflects the influence of the various religious traditions: 24 percent of Catholics and only 11 percent of Protestants say a person trying to follow Jesus should receive communion; 27 percent of Protestants and only 8 percent of Catholics said such a person should read the Bible daily.

The second difference involves evangelization: 31 percent of Protestants and only 12 percent of Catholics said a person trying to follow Jesus should tell other people about Jesus. Again and again we see this reluctance to evangelize on the part of Catholics. For example, in another survey, only 34 percent of Catholics say that "sharing the love of Christ with others" is "very important" to them, compared to 51 percent of Protestants and 86 percent of Evangelicals. Similarly, only 41 percent of Catholics—compared to 57 percent of Protestants and 77 percent of Southern Baptists—said that they had ever encouraged anyone to believe in Jesus Christ or accept him as Savior. The aversion to evangelization among Catholics seems partly a result of a church tradition that has not emphasized evangelization in the way the Protestant churches have. But it also seems to reflect a particularly acute sense of respect for the religious views of others. This respect, in turn, is related to Catholic beliefs about salvation.

No area of our findings better supports the notion that Catholics are —literally—more "down-to-earth" in their beliefs than that of attitudes toward personal salvation. In short, while salvation is a top priority, perhaps the top priority for Protestants, it is a much lower priority for Catholics. A 1978 study conducted for *Christianity Today* found that while Protestants rated salvation first on a list of personal needs, Catholics listed it fourth. Methodists showed a pattern similar to that of Catholics, while Baptists and Lutherans were closer to the Protestant pattern.

Catholic		*Protestant*	
1. PHYSICAL WELL-BEING/ HEALTH	27	SALVATION—CLOSENESS TO GOD	28
2. LOVE AND AFFECTION	19	PHYSICAL WELL-BEING/ HEALTH	24

Catholic		Protestant	
3. PURPOSE—A SENSE OF MEANING IN LIFE	15	LOVE AND AFFECTION	15
4. SALVATION—CLOSENESS TO GOD	14	PURPOSE—A SENSE OF MEANING IN LIFE	12

A separate survey found that Catholics are less likely than Protestants—and considerably less likely than Evangelicals—to say that having eternal salvation is "very important" to them:

HAVING ETERNAL SALVATION

	Very important	Fairly important	Fairly unimportant	Not at all important
EVANGELICAL	95	4	—	1
SOUTHERN BAPTIST	79	7	9	5
BAPTIST	74	17	4	5
PROTESTANT	69	18	7	4
METHODIST	65	21	7	5
CATHOLIC	56	28	10	3

The *Christianity Today* study also tells us that there are substantial differences between Catholics and Protestants in their views on Heaven: While almost nine in ten in both groups believe in some form of life after death, they differ sharply on what one must do to achieve it. Some 43 percent of Catholics believe that: "Heaven is a divine reward for those who earn it by their good life," double the percentage of Protestants choosing that answer. At the same time, 59 percent of Protestants —double the percentage of Catholics—say: "The only hope for Heaven is through personal faith in Jesus Christ." The stereotype that Catholics believe Heaven is achieved by good works and Protestants believe it is achieved by faith is clearly borne out by this finding.

1. *There is no life after death.*
2. *There is life after death, but what a person does in this life has no bearing on it.*
3. *Heaven is a divine reward for those who earn it by their good life.*
4. *The only hope for Heaven is through personal faith in Jesus Christ.*

	1.	2.	3.	4.
CATHOLIC	9	13	43	31
PROTESTANT	7	8	20	59
SOUTHERN BAPTIST	8	5	13	72
BAPTIST	8	7	16	66
METHODIST	7	13	20	55
LUTHERAN	6	12	18	58

But while Catholics differ in their beliefs about how they will get to Heaven, they hold identical views on whether or not they will get there —two thirds of both groups say their chances of going to Heaven are "excellent" or "good."

Catholic attitudes toward another aspect of salvation pose a sharp contrast to those of Protestants: the sensitive question of whether a non-Christian can go to Heaven. Catholics are 25 percentage points more likely than Protestants to say that a person who does not accept Jesus can have everlasting life; while Protestants reject this notion almost three to one (63–23 percent), a plurality of Catholics (48–37 percent) believe non-Christians can go to Heaven. (The one exception is generally liberal Episcopalians, who are even a little more likely than Catholics to say that non-Christians can go to Heaven.) Catholic attitudes on this question suggest greater tolerance of Jews and nonbelievers.

DO YOU THINK THAT A PERSON WHO DOES NOT ACCEPT JESUS CAN HAVE EVERLASTING LIFE?

	Yes	No
EPISCOPALIAN	52	35
CATHOLIC	48	37
PRESBYTERIAN	38	51
LUTHERAN	28	55
METHODIST	27	56
PROTESTANT	23	63
BAPTIST	13	73
SOUTHERN BAPTIST	11	76

THE BIBLE

The Bible has long been at the heart of religious differences between Catholics and Protestants. At the risk of oversimplifying: for Protestants, the Bible is the supreme religious authority; for Catholics, the supreme religious authority is the tradition of the Church as symbolized in the papacy. Pope John Paul II summarized Catholic teaching on the Bible before a general audience on April 24, 1985:

"Christ commanded his apostles to proclaim the Good News of salvation. The apostles did this by handing on, through their preaching and example, what they themselves had received. Some apostles and others associated with them committed the message to writing. Moreover, in order that the Gospel might always be preserved in the Church, the apostles chose bishops as their successors, giving them their own teaching authority.

"The Word of God is expressed and preserved in sacred tradition and in the inspired books of the Old and New Testaments. Tradition transmits in its entirety the Word of God which has been entrusted by Christ and his Spirit to the apostles and their successors. Sacred Scripture is the Word of God as it is put down in writing, under the inspiration of the Holy Spirit. The Church does not draw her certainty about revealed truths from the Bible alone. Sacred tradition and sacred Scripture make up a single deposit of the Word of God which is entrusted to the Church.

"The task of giving an authentic interpretation of the Word of God has been committed to the living teaching office of the Church, which is exercised in the name of Jesus Christ. This teaching office is not superior to the Word of God but is its servant, since it teaches only what has been handed on to it.

"Tradition, sacred Scripture and the teaching office of the Church—together with a supernatural appreciation of the faith by the whole people of God who have accepted the Word of God faithfully transmitted in its purity and integrity—form that living process in which divine revelation is passed on to new generations of believers." *(NC News Service)*

The Catholic Church does not teach belief in the Bible as the literal Word of God. It speaks of the Bible as "inspired" and sees no contradiction between modern methods of biblical scholarship and the sacred nature of the Bible. That view of biblical scholarship, together with the emphasis on interpretation of the Bible by church authorities, provides a strong Catholic context for biblical interpretation. One would expect, therefore, that Catholics would be more likely than Protestants to view the Bible as the "inspired Word of God," rather than the "literal Word of God"—and that is exactly what we did find in a 1985 survey:

BELIEFS ABOUT THE BIBLE

	Literal Word of God	Inspired Word of God	Book of fables
SOUTHERN BAPTIST	54	37	6
BAPTIST	53	37	6
PROTESTANT	47	43	7
METHODIST	38	49	10
CATHOLIC	32	53	8

We see that a majority of Catholics view the Bible as "inspired" and a plurality of Protestants view it as "literal." Significantly, however, we also see that Baptists are most likely to view the Bible as "literal," while Methodists, who would be fairly typical of mainline Protestant denominations, are closer to Catholics in viewing the Bible as "inspired." Here, Catholics and mainline Protestants are closer to each other than either are to Evangelical Christians, as typified by Baptists.

Interestingly enough, however, the 32 percent of Catholics who said they believed the Bible is "the literal Word of God" showed an increase of 6 percentage points since 1982; this could simply reflect the statistical margin of error in the two surveys, but it raises the possibility of a resurgence of Catholic fundamentalism. Of course, we suspect that believing in the Bible as the "literal Word of God" still means something different for Catholics than it does for Southern Baptists, but it is nonetheless a trend worth watching closely in the future.

Given the difference in Catholic and Protestant views about the Bible itself, it is not surprising that there is also difference on a key issue involving the Bible: creation. Fundamentalist Christians hold that life began as it was described in the Bible, with the creation of Adam and Eve; they view the biological process of evolution as a rejection of the biblical. Catholics take a different view. Since the 1940s, the Catholic Church has taught that the Bible is a religious book, not a book of natural history, and that a belief in evolution does not necessarily contradict the Bible. Pope Pius XII took this position in his 1950 encyclical *Humani Generis*. Pope John Paul II reaffirmed this view in April 1985, when he told a symposium on evolution and the Bible: "Evolution is not blocked by faith if discussion of it remains in the context of the naturalistic method and its possibilities."

Our surveys do show that Catholics are more likely to believe in evolution with God than in creationism, while Protestants are more likely to believe in creationism. At the same time, while Catholic-Protestant differences on this issue are significant, the size of the Catholic group supporting creationism is surprising, given church teaching. But, again, there is no evidence that Catholics who believe in creationism approach the issue in the same way as Fundamentalist Creationists.

CREATIONISM

	Creationism	Evolution with God	Evolution without God
CATHOLIC	38	47	8
PROTESTANT	49	36	7
TOTAL	44	38	9

One dimension of the Catholic pragmatism reflected in its "this-worldly" orientation is a more communal emphasis. This is also related to the communal nature of the Church. The Catholic Church has always had a sense of group identity about it; this has been reinforced by its traditional emphasis on family life. This communal dimension has been particularly reinforced in the United States by the sense of ethnic identity found in so many American Catholics.

Catholic Church leaders have expressed concern that American Catholics have taken on an individualistic nature usually found among Protestants. There is no doubt that American Catholics do have a strong individualistic streak. But they do still exhibit a pattern of communal concern. This can be seen in responses to a request to choose the top priority for Christians:

TOP PRIORITY FOR CHRISTIANS

A. *Help to win the world for Jesus Christ.*
B. *Concentrate on the spiritual growth of one's family and self.*
C. *Support causes to improve entire community.*

D. *Strengthen local church.*

E. *Influence local, state, and national legislatures on important issues.*

	A.	B.	C.	D.	E.
CATHOLIC	18	43	17	7	7
PROTESTANT	35	37	12	6	4
EVANGELICAL	62	26	4	5	2
BAPTIST	40	31	12	9	5
SOUTHERN BAPTIST	42	30	8	5	11
METHODIST	25	45	15	4	6

We see that Catholics and Protestants both pick the spiritual growth of themselves and their families as the top priority for Christians. But Protestants are just as likely to choose helping to win the world for Christ as their top priority; they are three times as likely to pick that as to pick working for causes to help the whole community. Catholics, on the other hand, are equally likely to pick those two choices, giving a proportionately higher emphasis on serving the whole community.

A related question asks whether the Christian must love God first, love his or her neighbor first, or love both equally. Here, again, Catholics show a more communal orientation—one in three Catholics say they should love their neighbor first or equally with God, while only one Protestant in five shares this view, again with the notable exception of Episcopalians.

	Love God first	Love neighbor first	Love both equally
EVANGELICAL	85	3	13
BAPTIST	76	4	15
LUTHERAN	74	9	11
PROTESTANT	74	7	14
PRESBYTERIAN	69	12	18
METHODIST	67	10	17
EPISCOPALIAN	60	16	16
NON-EVANGELICAL	59	13	18
CATHOLIC	59	11	23

CONCLUSION

Although we have compared Catholics and Protestants in this chapter and will continue to do so throughout, we would like to emphasize again that there is a need to redraw the map of American Christianity. There are two very distinct major divisions of American Protestantism: the mainline Protestants and the Evangelicals. On most issues of religious belief, Catholics and Evangelicals mark opposite poles within Christianity; if we were to draw a line halfway between them, mainline Protestants would, in the vast majority of cases, fall on the "Catholic" side of the line. Most of the Catholic-Protestant differences we have discussed still hold true for mainline Protestants, but not to the same degree as Catholic-Evangelical or overall Catholic-Protestant splits.

The Catholic-Protestant differences we have seen come in the context of virtually identical views on the existence of God, the divinity of Christ, and the existence of an afterlife. A major difference comes in what we have called the "intensity factor." While American Catholics have become increasingly comfortable with using the Protestant language about "personal relationships" with God and with Jesus, they have not internalized those terms and remain much less personal in their approach to religion.

This "intensity factor" reflects five significant Catholic-Protestant differences in religious belief:

- The Catholic approach is more intellectual in nature; this is reflected in the greater Catholic tendency to believe that the Bible is not meant to be interpreted literally, and in the greater Catholic acceptance of the compatability of evolution of physical life with the existence and creative power of God.

- The Catholic approach is more accepting; this is reflected in the fact that Catholics are less likely than Protestants to label many behaviors as sinful, in the fact that Catholics are more likely to believe that salvation is possible without belief in Christ, and in the fact that a significant minority of Catholics are more likely to say it is possible to be a good Christian without believing in the divinity of Christ.

- The Catholic approach is more pragmatic; Catholics give a relatively low priority to personal salvation and a higher priority to grappling with problems in this world.

■ The Catholic approach is more communal; Catholics are more likely to emphasize love of neighbor and to rank broader social concerns above personal evangelization.

■ The Catholic approach is more private; reflecting their more accepting worldview, Catholics are far less likely than Protestants to place a high priority on spreading their faith.

Protestant religiosity is "private" in its emphasis on the individual, but very "public" in its emphasis on bringing Christ to others. Catholics are just the opposite: They are less "private" in that they place a greater emphasis on the horizontal dimension of religion, but they are considerably more "private" in their indifference to evangelization. But if American Catholics seem relatively unconcerned about the outward dimensions of religion, they are, nevertheless, acting out a religion that views this world as holy.

III. RELIGIOUS PRACTICE

Just as Catholic patterns of religious belief differ from Protestant patterns, so do Catholic patterns of religious practice. Looking at measures of Bible reading or evangelization efforts, for example, will not produce an accurate picture of the state of Catholic religious practice, because Bible reading and evangelism have not traditionally had a high priority in Catholic life. The focal point of Catholic religious life is the weekly Mass. The Mass is important in itself—weekly attendance is required and the sacrament of the Eucharist is celebrated within the service. But Mass attendance is also important because it serves as a barometer of more general religious belief and practice. It is no surprise, then, that church leaders are so concerned about the dramatic decline in Mass attendance in recent decades. The U.S. bishops are studying ways to increase attendance, and Pope John Paul II has on several occasions urged American Catholics to be more observant in fulfilling their Mass obligation.

How much has Mass attendance declined among American Catholics? In 1958, 74 percent of Catholics said they had attended church in the past seven days; in 1985, 53 percent said they had attended in that period—a decline of 30 percent. In comparison, church attendance among Protestants fell less than 10 percent over the same length of time, from 44 percent in 1958 to 39 percent in 1985.

The decline in Mass attendance occurred in several stages. First, there was an erosion of 9 points, from 74 to 65 percent, between 1958 and 1968; then, a more dramatic decline of 13 points, from 65 to 52 percent, between 1968 and 1978; finally, there has been stability for a decade, with attendance ranging between 51 and 53 percent, a statistically insignificant difference, between 1978 and 1985.

But there are a number of indications that the decline in Mass atten-

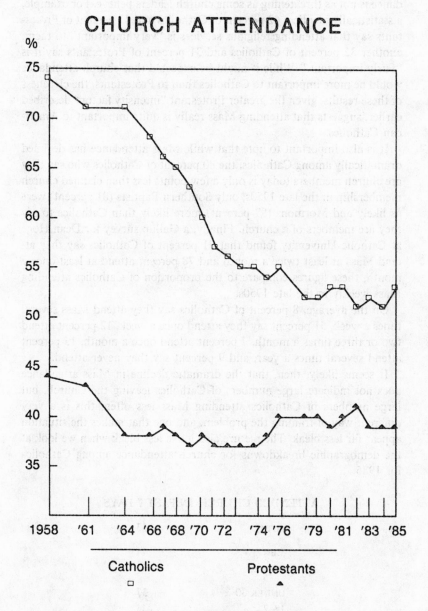

dance is not as threatening as some church leaders believe. For example, a statistically identical 42 percent of Catholics and 43 percent of Protestants say that attending religious services is "very important" to them; another 32 percent of Catholics and 31 percent of Protestants say it is "fairly important." While it might be expected that church attendance would be more important to Catholics than to Protestants, the closeness of these results, given the greater Protestant "intensity factor" described earlier, suggests that attending Mass really is quite important to American Catholics.

It is also important to note that while Mass attendance has declined dramatically among Catholics, the 80 percent of Catholics who say they are church members today is only a few points less than claimed church membership in the late 1950s; only Southern Baptists (81 percent) were as likely and Mormons (87 percent) more likely than Catholics to say they are members of a church. Finally, a Gallup survey for Dean Hoge at Catholic University found that 71 percent of Catholics say they attend Mass at least twice a month and 78 percent attend at least once a month; these figures compare to the proportion of Catholics attending Mass weekly in the late 1950s.

On the average, 8 percent of Catholics say they attend Mass several times a week, 51 percent say they attend once a week, 12 percent attend two or three times a month, 7 percent attend once a month, 13 percent attend several times a year, and 9 percent say they never attend.

It seems likely, then, that the dramatic decline in Mass attendance does not indicate large numbers of Catholics leaving the Church, but large numbers of Catholics attending Mass less often; this is a very different way of framing the problem, and one that makes the situation appear far less bleak. The picture also looks less bleak when we look at the demographic breakdowns for church attendance among Catholics for 1985:

ATTENDED CHURCH IN PAST 7 DAYS

TOTAL	53
MEN	44
WOMEN	61
UNDER 30	37
18–24	36
25–29	39

30–49	54
OVER 50	67
50–64	64
OVER 65	71
EAST	49
MIDWEST	59
SOUTH	54
WEST	50
COLLEGE GRADUATE	61
COLLEGE INCOMPLETE	55
HIGH SCHOOL GRADUATE	47
LESS THAN H.S. GRAD.	53
$40,000 +	53
$35–40,000	52
$25–35,000	45
$15–25,000	53
$10–15,000	63
UNDER $10,000	50

First, given the widespread discussion of the discontent of Catholic women with the Church today, it is rather surprising to find that 61 percent of Catholic women attended church within a seven-day period. There is a considerable "gender gap" here, but the 44 percent of men who attended Mass in a week is still higher than the national average for Protestants.

As expected, Mass attendance increases with age—a full seven in ten Catholics over sixty-five attend church in a given week. The 37 percent of Catholics aged eighteen to twenty-nine who attended church is obviously low, but it still compares favorably with the national average for Protestants. Further, the slight increase from 36 to 39 percent attendance among those aged twenty-five through twenty-nine suggests that the "homecoming effect," in which young adults return to the Church as they grow older and begin to raise families, is at work among young Catholics. A rather startling finding is the 61 percent of college graduates who said they had attended Mass within the week; this is one indicator that educated Catholics are more, not less, satisfied with their church.

While Mass attendance among Catholics has remained stable for the past decade, there has been a dramatic—and perhaps surprising—increase in religious activity outside of church. In early 1986 we repeated a question from a 1977 survey conducted for the Catholic Press Association that asked Catholics what religious activities they had participated in within the past thirty days. We found an increase in ten of eleven activities:

	1977	1986	Change
SAID (PRAYED) THE ROSARY	36	38	+ 2
MEDITATED	32	39	+ 7
READ THE BIBLE	23	32	+ 9
ATTENDED CATHOLIC SOCIAL FUNCTION	21	33	+ 12
GONE TO CONFESSION	18	23	+ 5
ATTENDED MEETING OF CATHOLIC ORGANIZATION	10	17	+ 7
ATTENDED A PRAYER MEETING	8	12	+ 4
PARTICIPATED IN CATHOLIC ACTION OR OUTREACH PROGRAM	4	7	+ 3
ATTENDED MARRIAGE ENCOUNTER SESSION	3	2	− 1
ATTENDED A SPIRITUAL CONFERENCE	2	3	+ 1
MADE A RETREAT	2	4	+ 2
ATTENDED RELIGIOUS EDUCATION CLASS		5	
ATTENDED BIBLE STUDY GROUP		5	
BEEN INVOLVED IN EVANGELIZING OTHERS		3	
TAKEN PART IN CHARISMATIC RENEWAL		4	
TAKEN PART IN RENEWAL PROGRAM		4	
NONE	31	23	− 8

Slightly different wording in the question does not affect the net results. We can see further evidence of this increased activity by adding the total percentages for the specified activities. In 1977, the total was 159 percent (obviously greater than 100 percent, because many people engage in more than one activity). In 1986, the same activities total 210 percent. In 1977, this averaged out to 2.3 activities per person; in 1986, it averaged 2.7 activities per person. In other words, there has been an increase in both the number of Catholics taking part in religious activities outside of church and in the number of activities in which they are taking part.

What accounts for these increases? In some ways, they represent the

Catholic manifestation of the moderate religious revival taking place in America and affecting Protestants and Jews as well. But there are also some uniquely Catholic factors involved. One is the fact that in 1977 the Church was led by an ill and aging Pope Paul VI, who died the next year. When Paul's immediate successor, Pope John Paul I, died after only a month in office, the College of Cardinals elected a young, energetic Pole, Cardinal Karol Wojtyla, as Pope. Wojtyla, who took the name John Paul II, has proved to be a popular figure, almost a folk hero, and his leadership has reinvigorated the Church.

We offer another, more controversial reason for the increase in Catholic religious and devotional activity. When the U.S. bishops engaged in the process of writing pastoral letters on peace and economic justice, some critics charged that they would be better served by paying more attention to more "churchy" matters. But as the bishops became more involved in the pastoral process, particularly with the peace pastoral, they noticed an interesting response—a renewed enthusiasm about the Church itself. Bishop Kenneth Untener, of Saginaw, Michigan, told the bishops in November 1982 that "alienated Catholics see in this a call to come home to a Church of which they are very proud." It is entirely possible that by addressing a "nonchurchy" issue of direct concern to Catholics in their daily lives, the threat of nuclear destruction, and by consulting their own people as well as experts in the process, the U.S. bishops did, in fact, cause American Catholics to take a new pride in their Church—a pride that manifested itself partly through increased religious activity.

Some of the 1986 findings indicate a remarkable amount of consistency. For example, a 1971 Gallup Poll for *Newsweek* found that 40 percent of Catholics had prayed the rosary in the past four weeks— down from the level of the 1950s but identical to the percentage today. In 1971, 24 percent of Catholics said they had gone to confession in the past eight weeks; the 23 percent who said in 1986 that they had gone in the past thirty days represents a real increase over the earlier result. This increase contradicts the impression of church leaders that there has been a dramatic decline in confession in recent years; it may well be argued that the percentage of Catholics going to confession should be higher, but these figures do not justify the conclusion that a dramatic decline in confession has taken place. There is even further reason for optimism—our figures show a slight increase in confession among Catholics under thirty, from 12 percent in 1977 to 14 percent in 1986. This increase is within the margin of error, but the increase in other religious practices by young Catholic adults supports the likelihood that there was an actual increase in confession by Catholics under thirty.

In general, some of the sharpest differences in religious practices came across age lines. While only 12 percent of those over fifty had not taken part in any of the listed activities, the figure was 25 percent for those between thirty and forty-nine and 35 percent for those aged eighteen to twenty-nine. In a few areas, there was no difference across age groups; the most surprising was Bible reading, with 32 percent of those aged eighteen to twenty-nine, 31 percent of those between thirty and forty-nine, and 38 percent of those over fifty saying they had read the Bible in the past thirty days. On praying the rosary, meditating, going to confession, and involvement in Catholic organizational activity, young people were consistently underrepresented:

DIFFERENCE IN KEY RELIGIOUS PRACTICES BY AGE

	18–29	30–49	50 +
PRAYED THE ROSARY	28	29	59
MEDITATED	20	44	52
GONE TO CONFESSION	14	21	34
ATTENDED CATHOLIC SOCIAL FUNCTION	22	34	41

But, as with confession, there has been a dramatic increase in religious practice by young Catholics; the percentage of Catholics under thirty saying they had not taken part in any religious activity during the past thirty days dropped from 41 percent in 1977 to 35 percent in 1986. The total participation in the 1977 activities was 110 percent; for the same activities in 1986, it was 156 percent. This amounts to a jump from 1.9 activities per person in 1977 to 2.4 per person in 1986.

RELIGIOUS ACTIVITY BY CATHOLICS 18–29

	1977	1986	Change
READ THE BIBLE	17	32	+ 15
PRAYED THE ROSARY	24	28	+ 4
MEDITATED	23	20	− 3
GONE TO CONFESSION	12	14	+ 2
ATTENDED CATHOLIC SOCIAL FUNCTION	16	22	+ 6
ATTENDED MEETING OF CATHOLIC ORGANIZATION	6	12	+ 6

	1977	1986	Change
ATTENDED PRAYER MEETING	5	15	+ 10
MADE A RETREAT	1	4	+ 3
ATTENDED SPIRITUAL CONFERENCE	1	3	+ 2
PARTICIPATED IN CATHOLIC SOCIAL ACTION	1	4	+ 3
OR OUTREACH PROGRAM			
ATTENDED MARRIAGE ENCOUNTER SESSION	4	2	− 2

As we examine our findings on religious activity more closely, some interesting patterns emerge. For example, we find an unusual regional pattern by comparing the total activity percentages for four regions with the national average. The East, with a total activity percentage of 191 percent, ranks at the bottom among the four regions; the Midwest, with 283 percent, ranks at the top, followed by the West (260 percent) and the South (252 percent).

We see that the East ranks below the national average and well below the other regions in religious activity. The Midwest, traditionally regarded as the center of progressive Catholicism in America, shows the highest level of religious activity. The conventional wisdom in many Catholic circles today is that the East is the area of the most conservative church leadership, while the other areas are more progressive. If that is in fact the case, it may well be that, contrary to the conventional wisdom, it is progressive, not conservative, church leadership that spurs more grass-roots devotional activity.

The "gender gap" in religious practice among Catholics is surprisingly small. The only area in which there was a statistically significant difference between the practices of men and women was in Bible reading, with women, following a national pattern, more likely than men to read the Bible. At the same time, 30 percent of men and only 18 percent of women said they had not been involved in any of the activities listed; but the difference in Bible reading alone could account for much of this difference. We have already seen that men make up a higher percentage of Catholics than of most Protestant denominations.

Education is less of a factor than might be expected in determining the degree of religious activity. There is little difference in behavior between those who have graduated high school and those who have gone to college, but both groups are considerably more active than those with only a grade school education: 24 percent of those with some college, 22 percent of those with a high school education, and 33 percent of those with a grade school education had not been involved in any listed activities. The biggest differences by education groups came in methods of prayer: Those with grade school education were more likely to pray the rosary, while those with college education were more likely to meditate. N.B.: participation in both Bible reading and confession were consistent across all education levels.

Another important finding is that two overlapping groups—those over fifty and those in households in which the chief wage earner is not in the labor force (largely retired workers)—constantly show up among those most involved in a wide variety of activities, from private activities like meditating and praying the rosary to more social activities such as attending meetings of Catholic organizations, taking part in Catholic action or outreach, or evangelizing others. This is partly a reflection of the fact that older Americans in general are more religious than others; also, many have more free time because they are retired and/or their children have grown up and left home. But these findings suggest that Catholics over fifty and those in the non-labor force may be an untapped resource for church leadership.

Finally, another pattern which emerges is that people from different backgrounds get involved in different activities. For example, those with incomes below $10,000 a year are more likely than the average to pray the rosary, read the Bible, and go to confession, while those with incomes above $50,000 a year are more likely to meditate and to be involved in Catholic organizations and social functions.

CATHOLICS AND THE BIBLE

Because the Bible does not occupy the same priority for Catholics that it does for Protestants, it is not surprising that fewer Catholics than Protestants read the Bible and that those who do, read it less regularly. A variety of findings support the conclusion that Catholics place a far lower priority on the Bible than do Protestants:

- In a 1984 survey, 21 percent of Catholics, 52 percent of Protestants, and 85 percent of Evangelicals said that reading or studying the Bible was "very important" to them; 28 percent of Catholics, 12 percent of Protestants, and 2 percent of Evangelicals said reading or studying the Bible was "not very important" to them.
- While the percentage of Protestants and Evangelicals participating

in Bible study rose between 1982 and 1985, the percentage of Catholics involved held steady at 9 percent.

■ Twenty-four percent of Catholics, 52 percent of Protestants, and 73 percent of Evangelicals say they turn to the Bible first when they feel a need to "nourish" their faith.

■ While the level of biblical illiteracy is high among all Americans, it is particularly high among Catholics. For example: only 31 percent of Catholics, 59 percent of Protestants, and 69 percent of Evangelicals could name Matthew, Mark, Luke, and John as the four Gospels of the New Testament; only 38 percent of Catholics, 46 percent of Protestants, and 57 percent of Evangelicals could identify the person who delivered the Sermon on the Mount as Jesus.

Given this pattern, the increase among Catholics of those who said they read the Bible within the past thirty days from 23 to 32 percent between 1977 and 1986 suggests that Catholics are taking a closer look at the Bible. Those Catholics more likely than the average to read the Bible include women, Westerners, blacks, low-income and low-education groups, and those in the non-labor force. Least likely to read the Bible are men, Easterners, professional and business people, and those with incomes above $50,000 a year. But there has been an increase in Bible reading in virtually all groups of Catholics.

The Bible has been drawn into the center of Catholic life since the Second Vatican Council, which declared, in *The Dogmatic Constitution on Divine Revelation,* that: "Access to sacred Scripture ought to be opened wide to the Christian faithful." The Council made several important changes regarding the Bible. First, it reordered Bible readings at Mass to provide a more representational sample of passages throughout the year. Second, it required that homilies at Mass be based on the Scripture passage of the day.

"The new emphasis on Scripture-based homilies contributed to a far greater appreciation of the Bible among Catholics than before," Bishop James Malone, of Youngstown, Ohio, president of the National Conference of Catholic Bishops, said in a report prepared for the 1985 extraordinary synod marking the twentieth anniversary of the closing of the Council. "Catholics in the United States are now more familiar with the Bible than ever before and have a greater appreciation of the centrality of the Word of God in Catholic life and worship."

PRAYER

Prayer is more central than Bible reading to the Catholic tradition, and this is reflected in a number of survey findings. For example, the gap between Catholics and Protestants among those saying prayer is "very important" to them is only 10 points: 58 percent for Catholics and 68 percent for Protestants. Ninety-four percent of Evangelicals say prayer is "very important." Similarly, 58 percent of Catholics, 67 percent of Protestants, and 76 percent of Evangelicals turn to individual prayer to nourish their faith.

Catholics are as likely (93 percent) as Protestants (92 percent) to say they've prayed within the past seven days. But there are significant differences within that period. For example, 59 percent of Catholics, 49 percent of Protestants, and 38 percent of Evangelicals said they had prayed once a day or less during the past week; 11 percent of Catholics, 20 percent of Protestants, and 36 percent of Evangelicals said they had prayed three times a day or more.

There are other Catholic-Protestant differences related to prayer:

▪ Catholics are the most likely group to say they never turned to quiet prayer in the past year and the least likely to say they did so "many" times:

TURNED TO QUIET PRAYER IN THE PAST YEAR

	Never	Once	Several times	Many times
CATHOLIC	30	8	39	23
PROTESTANT	21	5	41	32
EVANGELICAL	8	2	47	44

▪ Catholics are not likely to turn to prayer groups: 16 percent of Catholics, 24 percent of Protestants, and 39 percent of Evangelicals said they turn to prayer groups to nourish their faith.

▪ Catholics are considerably less dramatic than Protestants in their reaction to prayer. Here, again, they are much closer in behavior to mainline Protestants than to Evangelicals. For example, Evangelicals are twice as likely as Catholics to say that God told them what to do after they prayed. Catholics are also closer to mainline Protestants in the way that prayer affects their decision making; they are considerably less likely than Evangelicals to take action after praying:

AFTER PRAYER

1. *God told you what to do in prayer.*
2. *Became calmer in prayer.*
3. *Took some action because of prayer.*
4. *Attitude changed because of prayer.*
5. *Transformed because of prayer.*

	1.	*2.*	*3.*	*4.*	*5.*
EVANGELICAL	71	95	72	87	71
BAPTIST	61	90	64	79	59
PROTESTANT	50	88	57	77	46
METHODIST	44	86	51	76	38
LUTHERAN	39	79	42	71	37
CATHOLIC	36	78	45	64	34
EPISCOPALIAN	33	84	53	76	24
PRESBYTERIAN	27	66	35	46	17

The difference in Catholic and Protestant religious styles is reflected in response to a question about where people turn to nourish or strengthen their faith. (See Appendix.) Catholics place a higher priority on attending religious services and receiving communion. While reading the Bible to nourish faith has a high priority among Protestants, Catholics rank it seventh, just behind turning to nature.

TO NOURISH FAITH: RANKINGS

	Catholics	*Protestants*	*Evangelicals*
1.	PRAYER ALONE	PRAYER ALONE	PRAYER ALONE
2.	RELIGIOUS SERVICES/HELPING OTHERS	HELPING OTHERS	READ THE BIBLE
3.	COMMUNION	READ THE BIBLE	HELPING OTHERS
4.	SERMONS/LECTURES	RELIGIOUS SERVICES	RELIGIOUS SERVICES
5.	MEDITATION	SERMONS/LECTURES	SERMONS/LECTURES

Catholics	*Protestants*	*Evangelicals*
6. NATURE	MEDITATION	MEDITATION
7. READ THE BIBLE	NATURE	PRAYER GROUP/ COMMUNION

The privacy that American Catholics feel about their faith is reflected in their cautious attitude toward evangelizing others. For example, only 34 percent of Catholics say that "sharing the love of Christ with others" is "very important" to them, compared to 51 percent of Protestants and 86 percent of Evangelicals. Similarly, only 41 percent of Catholics— compared to 57 percent of Protestants and 77 percent of Southern Baptists—said that they had ever encouraged anyone to believe in Jesus Christ or accept him as Savior. In our 1986 survey, only 3 percent of Catholics said they had been active in evangelizing others in the past thirty days. While the margin of error for figures in this range is quite large, it does seem that some groups seem a bit more interested in evangelization than others—notably blacks, Southerners, those in the non-labor force, those with incomes between $10,000 and $15,000 a year, and those with some college. Those least likely to evangelize were Easterners, those with no college, and those with incomes below $10,000 a year.

The Protestant emphasis on individual charity and involvement is responsible for a gap between Catholics and Protestants in volunteer work in both the church and the community. In one survey, for example, 34 percent of Protestants and only 28 percent of Catholics said they had been involved in charitable activities during the past year. Catholics also lagged well behind Protestants in several other areas of volunteer work as described in a survey done for Robert Schuller. Again, Catholics are much closer to mainline Protestants than to Evangelicals.

For example, 68 percent of Catholics say they did no volunteer work for the Church in the previous year; the figure for Protestants was 53 percent, and only 38 percent of Evangelicals said they had not volunteered for church work. Differences were smaller in two other areas. First, 65 percent of Catholics, 60 percent of Protestants, and 61 percent of Evangelicals said they had not volunteered to help their communities in the previous year. Second, 33 percent of Catholics, 27 percent of Protestants, and 21 percent of Evangelicals said they had not volunteered to help others in the past year.

Another form of church involvement in which Catholics lag well behind Protestants is financial support. The concept of tithing—giving one tenth of your income to your church—has never caught on among Catholics the way it has among Protestants, particularly Evangelicals: Only 8 percent of Catholics give 10 percent or more of their income to the Church, while 22 percent of Protestants tithe. Baptists (28 percent) and Southern Baptists (37 percent) are the most likely to tithe, with mainline Protestants ranking much lower, yet still ahead of Catholics:

	10% or more	5–9%	Less than 5%	Nothing
SOUTHERN BAPTIST	37	10	31	17
BAPTIST	28	14	29	20
PROTESTANT	22	14	29	22
LUTHERAN	15	18	30	20
METHODIST	12	15	36	23
CATHOLIC	8	14	46	21

RELIGIOUS TELEVISION

For the past decade, Catholic church leaders have been concerned about the number of Catholics watching and contributing to fundamentalist television evangelists. They view the evangelists as offering a theology markedly at odds with Catholicism and draining off funds that might otherwise be used for church purposes. A 1983 Gallup Poll, conducted as part of a major study of religious television commissioned by groups including the U.S. Catholic Conference, the National Council of Churches, National Religious Broadcasters, and a number of individual televangelists, produced several important findings. In general, while millions of American Catholics do in fact view and contribute to television evangelists, they do so in numbers considerably lower than their proportion of the general population.

Thirty-two percent of Americans said they had watched religious TV in the past month; Catholics make up 28 percent of the general population but only 19 percent of religious TV viewers and only 11 percent of those who have watched two or more hours of religious TV in the past week. In contrast, Protestants, who make up 58 percent of the population, account for 72 percent of religious TV viewers and 83 percent of those who watched two or more hours of religious TV in the past week.

The percentage of Catholics who contribute to religious television is even lower than the percentage of Catholics who watch it—Catholics make up only 14 percent of contributors; they make up 20 percent of viewers who do not contribute. Nearly one third of religious TV viewers made financial contributions to a program; the median amount contributed was $30 over the past year.

The profile of Catholics who watch religious TV is similar to that of Protestant viewers: They are older, less educated, more rural, disproportionately nonwhite and female, and more socially isolated; many are pretty much confined to their homes by age or health problems. In terms of their opinions, 50 percent of religious TV viewers said they were "very dissatisfied" with "the way moral standards have been changing in America," compared to 31 percent among nonviewers.

Only 3 percent of religious television viewers say viewing has decreased their church involvement. But one in six say that religious TV contributes more than their church to their spiritual life and one in three (34 percent) say this about religious TV's contribution to information on social and moral issues.

Given a list of eleven statements expressing some degree of dissatisfaction with their church, viewers and nonviewers on the whole held remarkably similar views about the Church—similar in not expressing a great deal of satisfaction. About four in ten in both groups said none of the statements was true. On specific statements, the difference between the two groups was never more than two percentage points. The only exception was that fewer viewers than nonviewers agreed with the statement: "I object to some of the things that my church or synagogue teaches." It appears doubtful, then, that dissatisfaction with local churches accounts for much of the reason why people watch religious television.

PERCEPTIONS OF THE CHURCH

	Viewers	Nonviewers
I object to some of the things my church teaches.	12	18
It isn't convenient for me to attend religious services.	13	13
I don't feel comfortable with the people at my church or synagogue.	9	8
I am dissatisfied with the pastor or rabbi at my church or synagogue.	5	6

	Viewers	Nonviewers
My local church or synagogue doesn't meet my spiritual needs.	9	8
Other responsibilities keep me from getting to religious services.	20	18
There is too much emphasis on money at my church or synagogue.	21	23
My local church or synagogue is too conservative on social issues.	6	8
My local church or synagogue is too liberal on social issues.	4	3
My local church or synagogue isn't addressing the serious issues currently facing our society.	10	8
I don't like the way services have changed at my church or synagogue.	9	10
Other	1	2
None	44	42

An examination of the viewing habits of Catholics who do watch religious television shows that Catholics are more likely to watch local programs, which are more often church services, than the major TV evangelists; not surprisingly, Jimmy Swaggart, who has called Catholicism a "false religion," draws an audience that is only 6 percent Catholic.

AUDIENCES FOR SPECIFIC PROGRAMS

	Billy Graham	Jimmy Swaggart	Oral Roberts	700 Club	Local Programs
CATHOLIC	17	6	14	18	24
PROTESTANT	81	83	80	71	68

Catholics also view the leading TV evangelists as considerably more conservative than they view themselves. On this scale, "1" is the most conservative position and "6" is the most liberal:

RELIGIOUS VIEWS

	1	2	3	4	5	6
JERRY FALWELL	23	11	7	4	5	2
ORAL ROBERTS	21	11	12	8	7	6
BILLY GRAHAM	19	16	14	14	9	5
JIMMY SWAGGART	9	7	8	5	5	2
PAT ROBERTSON	7	5	8	7	2	3
ROBERT SCHULLER	6	9	11	5	4	3
CATHOLIC	5	8	21	31	9	9

CONCLUSION

The conventional wisdom is that the level of religious participation is low and declining. The conventional wisdom is wrong.

While church attendance among Catholics has declined dramatically since the 1950s, it has been stable for a decade and may even be about to inch up a bit. Catholics still lag behind Protestants in many areas of religious participation, but this reflects differences in beliefs between the two groups that account for the Protestant "intensity factor" we discussed earlier; at the same time, church attendance among Catholics is still significantly greater than church attendance among Protestants.

The fact is, American Catholics are in the middle of a religious revival:

■ There has been a significant increase in Catholic religious activity outside of Mass in the past decade; more Catholics are involved in activities such as confession, saying the rosary, and becoming involved in church social and organizational life, and individual Catholics are involved in more types of religious activity than a decade ago.

■ While Catholics under thirty still lag behind older Catholics in participation in religious activities, the increase in such activity among young Catholics has paralleled the increase among all Catholics.

■ Bible reading has increased dramatically among Catholics of all ages, prayer remains important to Catholics, and Catholics still go to confession and say the rosary in the same proportions they did in the early 1970s.

Catholic participation in religious practices may not be as widespread as it was in the 1950s, but it is more widespread and vital than it has been for at least a decade—and seems likely to continue to grow.

IV. CATHOLICS AND THEIR CHURCH

The Second Vatican Council redefined the Catholic Church as "the People of God"—and if that is the criterion, the Council has been a raving success in the United States. That is not to say that the Church has no imperfections or that its members are not aware of them. But the picture of American Catholics that emerges from our data is that of a group of people secure in their sense of identity as Catholics. In some ways, they are extremely upbeat; in other areas, they have some serious criticisms of the Church and some serious disagreements with church teaching. But neither criticisms nor disagreements have changed their sense of belonging to the Church, indeed their sense of ownership of the Church. They believe that their criticisms will eventually be heard, partly because they have institutionalized a sense of change. They don't even necessarily want the Church to change all of the teachings with which they disagree; they just want those teachings viewed as ideals which may seem impractical in the real world and from which they may dissent in conscience.

There are a number of signs of vitality among American Catholics. They have more confidence in the Church than in any other institution; two Catholics in three express either "a great deal" or "a lot" of confidence in the Church. Beyond that, 85 percent of Catholics said that their religious experience over their lifetimes had been an overall positive experience; only 4 percent said it had been an overall negative experience. Here, too, there was no significant difference between Catholics and Protestants.

Catholics are more optimistic than Protestants—including Evangelicals—about the future of Christianity: 81 percent of Catholics, 74 percent of Evangelicals, and 71 percent of all Protestants say they are optimistic.

OUTLOOK FOR CHRISTIANITY

	Very optimistic	Optimistic	Pessimistic	Very pessimistic
CATHOLIC	15	66	8	2
METHODIST	18	63	10	2
SOUTHERN BAPTIST	15	57	22	*
PROTESTANT	17	54	14	3
BAPTIST	19	53	11	5
EVANGELICAL	26	48	12	4

Some other signs of enthusiasm come from a Gallup survey conducted for the Study of Future Church Leadership for Dean Hoge at Catholic University. The survey asked Catholics to rate "the way the priests in your parish are handling their job." An astonishing 88 percent approved of the job their priests were doing; only 9 percent disapproved. The ten-to-one approval is not only a sign of enthusiasm among lay Catholics; it is a cause for a real boost in morale among overworked priests, who often feel unappreciated. More specifically, 50 percent of Catholics said their parish priests were "very understanding" in their ability to appreciate the parishioners' practical problems; 37 percent said their priests were "fairly understanding," and only 8 percent said they were "not very understanding." Finally, 29 percent rated their priests' sermons as "excellent" and 44 percent rated them as "good"; 20 percent rated them "fair" and only 4 percent rated them "poor." The same survey also found that Catholics reject by 55–39 percent the statement that: "Most priests don't expect the lay members to be leaders, just followers." In a 1982 survey, 74 percent of Catholics gave their priests an "A" or a "B" grade.

Catholics offer a more mixed reaction—and some surprises—when asked to rate the Church's handling of the needs of various groups within the Church.

CHURCH'S HANDLING OF NEEDS OF GROUPS

	Excellent	Good	Fair	Poor
YOUR OWN NEEDS	14	36	37	9
WOMEN	7	30	34	26
LAY PEOPLE IN THE CHURCH	14	39	35	6
SINGLE PEOPLE	6	24	47	15

	Excellent	Good	Fair	Poor
FAMILIES	19	39	29	10
ELDERLY	14	39	32	10
MINORITIES	9	32	32	17
NEW IMMIGRANTS	9	29	31	17
SEPARATED/DIVORCED/REMARRIED	6	24	32	31
MARRIAGE ANNULMENT PROCESS	6	21	31	29
POLITICS AND PUBLIC-POLICY ISSUES	6	21	41	22
VATICAN II CHANGES	12	35	31	15
RELATIONS WITH NON-CHRISTIANS	12	42	25	13

We can get further insight into Catholics' feelings about their church when we look at the way different groups of people rate the Church's handling of their own needs:

CHURCH'S HANDLING OF YOUR OWN NEEDS

	Excellent	Good	Fair	Poor
TOTAL	14	36	37	9
MEN	15	40	30	12
WOMEN	14	33	44	7
18–29	9	37	41	11
30–49	15	33	43	4
OVER 50	19	40	25	14
OVER 65	28	55	11	4
EAST	11	33	44	11
MIDWEST	21	40	26	8
SOUTH	15	25	46	9
WEST	10	49	33	6
WHITE	14	38	37	9
NONWHITE	15	21	43	23
COLLEGE	14	45	25	11
HIGH SCHOOL	9	30	49	8
GRADE SCHOOL	19	39	32	9

	Excellent	Good	Fair	Poor
REPUBLICAN	13	41	33	10
DEMOCRAT	17	34	38	8
INDEPENDENT	14	30	43	12
$35,000 +	14	38	34	5
$15,000–34,999	11	43	37	4
UNDER $15,000	19	28	38	16

We can draw a number of conclusions from these findings. First, the Church gets high ratings for its handling of the needs of families. This is not surprising, given the family-oriented emphasis of most parishes. Perhaps related is the high rating the Church receives for handling the needs of the elderly and the dramatically high rating that those over sixty-five give the Church for meeting their needs. It's quite likely that these findings indicate a greater degree of satisfaction with the Church among the elderly than might have been anticipated.

But there is a flip side to the Church's high ratings on dealing with families and the elderly—the low approval ratings for dealing with singles and young people. The percentage of Catholics who rate the Church's handling of the needs of single people as "fair" or "poor" is twice the percentage of those who rate it "excellent" or "good." Only 9 percent of Catholics under thirty rate the Church's handling of their needs as "excellent." (The lower rating of the Church by political Independents than by Republicans and Democrats reflects the fact that this is generally a younger group.) Young people are typically less attached to the Church than those over thirty, and low ratings of the Church among this group are fairly typical, but they also suggest that the Catholic Church is not doing enough to reach out to young adults. At the same time, there has been a growing consensus within the Church in recent years that it is not doing enough for the one Catholic in three who is single.

One of our most interesting findings involves the different perceptions men and women have of the Church. Men are more satisfied than women are with the way the Church responds to their needs. The Church gets poor marks for its treatment of women, with 34 percent of Catholics saying it does only a fair job and 26 percent—one in four— saying it does a poor job. Surprisingly, men are slightly more likely than women to say the Church is doing a poor job of handling the needs of women. Finally, while women are not as satisfied with the Church as men are, they cluster in the "fair" category—only 7 percent of women say the Church does a poor job of meeting their own needs.

What are we to make of this, particularly in light of the debate over what some have characterized as "angry Catholic women" in the Church today? One measure of the depth of feeling among Catholic women can be found in reaction to the U.S. bishops' decision to write a pastoral letter on women in the Church and society. After a number of nuns and women's groups argued that a group composed only of men could not credibly write a document about women, the bishops changed the thrust of the pastoral to women's concerns. Anger is a measure of intensity, and it is quite likely that many women who are dissatisfied with the Church are, in fact, angry about it. And there is no doubt that many women are dissatisfied with the Church. But it would be difficult to look at these data and conclude that Catholic women as a group are angry. The data suggest that many women who believe the Church does not respond well to women in general are more satisfied with the way their own parish treats them—women are three times as likely to give the Church a "poor" rating for its handling of women in general as for the way it meets their own needs. Put another way, women who feel dissatisfied with the Church's treatment of them as women are more satisfied with the Church's treatment of them as persons. There is no doubt that church leadership faces a major challenge in improving the treatment of women and the perception of the treatment of women in the Church, but the challenge does not seem to be insurmountable.

One of our most surprising findings was the poor ratings given the Church on its involvement in political and public-policy issues. Only 27 percent rated the Church "excellent" or "good" in this area; 22 percent rated it "poor." The ratings were low in just about every group of Catholics, although younger Catholics were somewhat more supportive. Significantly, there was no marked difference between Republicans and Democrats in rating the Church's performance, although Independents were somewhat more critical. This suggests that the bishops are perceived as either nonpartisan in their public positions—or as tilting toward the Republicans over the abortion issue by Democratic Catholics and tilting toward the Democrats on peace and economic issues by Republican Catholics.

Catholic disapproval of the Church's handling of political issues is reinforced by two findings from the Hoge study. First, Catholics were evenly divided, agreeing by 50–47 percent that: "Priests should not use the pulpit to discuss social issues." Second, they disagreed by 55–39 percent that: "Bishops should speak out on political issues like nuclear war and the economy."

These findings are somewhat at odds with the fact that, as we will see shortly, one third of Catholics want more guidance from the Church on the moral issues of the day. They also seem to be at odds with the enthusiasm with which the bishops' pastoral letter on peace—and particularly the broad consultation process they used in preparing it—were met. There are several possible explanations. One is simply that Catholics want to make up their own minds about political issues and do not want to hear from their church about them. It is also possible that Catholics react negatively to the word "political" in questions about church activity. It is likely that Catholics feel more positive than these responses suggest about the Church addressing the moral dimension of public issues such as abortion, peace, and the economy, but Catholics firmly reject any church action that smacks of partisan politics or any form of political manipulation. And, if that is the case, it is clear that the bishops have not convinced their people that they are not getting involved in street-level politics.

Another surprising finding is the degree to which Catholics with a college background are satisfied with the Church—59 percent give the Church an "excellent" or "good" rating in meeting their own needs. There is some overlap here with the fact that those with higher incomes are also more satisfied with the Church. Again, there is a flip side—nonwhite Catholics and those with incomes below $15,000 a year are considerably dissatisfied with the Church. All Catholics give the Church low marks for its handling of the needs of minorities and new immigrants. Our data indicate that white, affluent, middle-class families are quite happy with the Church, but that discontent grows the farther away one goes from that category.

We also see a repetition of a fascinating regional difference. Catholics in the East, where involvement in religious practice is low, are also dissatisfied with the Church's handling of their needs: 55 percent give the Church a "fair" or "poor" rating. Again, the Midwest is the most enthusiastic region: 61 percent give the Church an "excellent" or a "good" rating. Dissatisfaction in the South is comparable to that in the East; this may partly reflect a higher proportion of black Catholics in the South. But it does seem that the conservatism of the Church in the East is responsible for lower levels of satisfaction there, while the liberalism of the Church in the Midwest is responsible for the higher levels of satisfaction there. Something clearly seems to be going on regionally. For example, the population in the East and the Midwest is older than the population elsewhere, and older Catholics are more satisfied. This would suggest that Catholics in both the East and the Midwest would be more satisfied, but they're not. At the same time, older Catholics are the least satisfied with the way the Church has handled the implementation of Vatican II changes. This suggests that both the East and the Midwest would rank the Church lower on its handling of those changes. But, again, the Midwest is considerably more satisfied than the East with the Church's handling of Vatican II changes.

It is interesting that the Church receives very mixed marks on its handling of the Vatican II changes—47 percent rate it "excellent" or "good," 46 percent rate it "fair" or "poor." It is important to note that this is not a rating of the changes themselves, but of the job the Church has done in implementing them. The 1977 Gallup Catholic Press Association study found that Catholics approved of the Council's reforms by 67–23 percent. Since younger Catholics were even more in favor of the Council's reforms, the level of support is very likely even greater today. Our new findings seem to confirm what the U.S. bishops said in their report to the 1985 Extraordinary Synod of Bishops, called to commemorate the twentieth anniversary of the conclusion of the Council: The Church in the United States needs to do a much better job of educating its people about the Council's changes than it has in the past.

But the Church does receive high marks for its approach to one change mandated by the Council: broader participation by lay people in church life. In our survey, 53 percent of Catholics rated the Church "excellent" or "good" in handling the needs of lay people in the Church, and only 6 percent rated it "poor." As we shall see shortly, Catholics want even more lay participation and leadership in the Church, but they seem pleased with what has happened in this area in the twenty years since the end of Vatican II.

Another change spurred by Vatican II that has gone down very well with American Catholics was the opening to closer relations with other denominations and faiths. In the CPA study, 84 percent of Catholics agreed with the statement: "The Catholic Church should become more ecumenical, that is, should try to develop closer relations between Catholics and non-Catholics." In the 1986 survey, the Church's handling of relations with non-Christians received one of the best ratings, with 54 percent of Catholics giving it an "excellent" or "good" rating.

Yet another popular change brought about by Vatican II was the celebration of the Mass in the vernacular. There is considerable support, however, for allowing parishes to celebrate the Mass in Latin if they wish; in the Hoge study, 67 percent said it would help the Church to allow periodic celebrations of a Latin Mass if a local church desires, and only 4 percent said it would hurt the Church. The CPA study found that two Catholics in three favored allowing parishes to celebrate the old-style Latin Mass, which differs in form from the new Mass. But the percentage of Catholics supporting these options is far greater than the percentage seeking to make use of them; a survey conducted by the National Conference of Catholic Bishops found that very few people have requested the Latin Mass. High support for the option of either the new Mass in Latin or the old-style Latin Mass are just that: support for an option by a people to whom options and respect for other people's views are quite important.

Beyond doubt, the area in which the Church receives its worst rating is its treatment of separated, divorced, and remarried Catholics and the related rating of its marriage tribunal system for processing church annulments. Three Catholics in ten rated the Church poor in these areas, and the "fair–poor" ratings outnumbered the "excellent–good" ratings two-to-one. These findings reflect two different issues. One is the pastoral care extended to the separated, divorced, and remarried. The second is outright disagreement with the Church's teaching on divorce. In a 1971 *Newsweek*-Gallup poll, 60 percent of Catholics said that a divorced Catholic who remarries is not living in sin, while only 28 percent disagreed. In the CPA study, Catholics said, three-to-one—69–23 percent—that: "Divorced Catholics should be allowed to remarry in the Church." Again, younger Catholics felt even more strongly about the need for a change.

Divorce is not the only issue on which Catholics differ with Church teaching. The subject on which there is the greatest disagreement is the Church's ban on artificial means of birth control. A sizable majority of Catholics rejected the reaffirmation of that position immediately upon the release of *Humanae Vitae*, Pope Paul VI's encyclical, in 1968. In 1971, Catholics said by 58–31 percent that a good Catholic could ignore the Pope's condemnation of artificial birth control. In the 1977 CPA study, 73 percent said Catholics should be allowed to practice artificial means of birth control; eight in ten Catholics under fifty took this position. Some observers believe that *Humanae Vitae* has been responsible for declining church attendance, and it is clearly a major factor cited by unchurched Catholics. But the size of the Catholic population has grown since 1968, and the decline in Mass attendance has been stable for a decade. It is not likely that people are turning away from the Church today because of the birth control issue; more likely, they reject the Church's teaching, practice birth control as a matter of conscience, and go to church or not for other reasons.

But it would be accurate to conclude that the birth control issue has damaged the Church's credibility on other sex-related issues. A prime example is attitudes toward premarital sex. In 1969, 72 percent of American Catholics said they believed that premarital sex was morally wrong; 70 percent of Protestants said it was wrong. But by 1985, only 33 percent of Catholics said premarital sex was wrong—a 39-point decline in sixteen years. The shift in attitude among Catholics was even more dramatic than that among the rest of the population, which moved from 68–21 percent disapproval of premarital sex to 52–39 percent approval. Catholics shifted from being slightly more likely than Protestants to disapprove of premarital sex to being considerably more likely to approve—Catholics approved by 58–33 percent, Protestants disapproved by 48–46 percent. While Southern Baptists were the only major denomination to disapprove of premarital sex, mainline Protestant denominations were still not as permissive as Catholics on the issue:

PREMARITAL SEX WRONG

	Yes	No
SOUTHERN BAPTIST	53	41
PROTESTANT	48	46
BAPTIST	48	45
METHODIST	41	46
LUTHERAN	38	55
CATHOLIC	33	58

But permissive Catholic attitudes toward birth control and premarital sex do not extend to abortion; Catholics do seem to see abortion as a "life" issue, not a "sex" issue. The CPA study found that Catholics rejected by 47–44 percent the statement that "the Catholic Church should relax its standards forbidding all abortions under any circumstances." Among Catholics under thirty, 49 percent supported a change and 42 percent opposed. This obviously amounts to less than unqualified support for the Church's position on abortion, but it suggests that Catholics are willing to make exceptions to a ban on abortion in the "hard" cases but do not want to throw away the Church's basic position on abortion.

Responses to several other questions in the 1985 Hoge survey suggest that substantial minorities of Catholics either disagree with or are not aware of key elements of church teaching:

- 57 percent of Catholics believed it was a sin to miss Mass when they could easily have attended; 36 percent disagreed. This is virtually the same response as in 1971.

- 60 percent believe that, under certain conditions, the Pope is infallible on faith and morals; 25 percent disagree, and 15 percent are undecided.

- 66 percent believe that "Jesus directly handed over leadership of the Church to Peter and the popes"; 17 percent disagree, and 17 percent are undecided.

How do Catholics believe the Church can better serve them? A 1984 survey indicates that while Protestants want more spiritual guidance from their church, Catholics want more practical help. Catholics cite help in becoming more effective parents as the area in which they would most like help from the Church. The next-highest priorities for Catholics were help in approaching moral issues, help in putting their faith into practice, and help in deepening their relationship with Christ. In contrast, Protestants and Evangelicals gave a higher priority to deepening their relationship with Christ and lower priority to practical matters; they ranked help in becoming more effective parents fifth. This finding is a reflection of the basic pragmatism which is an essential part of the Catholic religious worldview.

	Catholic	Protestant	Evangelical
DEEPEN RELATIONSHIP WITH CHRIST	32	42	57
PUT FAITH INTO PRACTICE	33	44	56
HELP WITH PRAYER LIFE	19	22	28
COUNSELING WITH PRAYER	16	18	30
SHED LIGHT ON ISSUES	32	37	35
DEVELOP BETTER USE OF GIFTS	18	24	31
SERVE OTHERS BETTER	28	36	40
BE MORE EFFECTIVE PARENTS	38	32	34

A Gallup survey conducted for Dean Hoge at Catholic University shows that the vast majority of Catholics also want more frequent informal relationships between priests and lay members and more small groups within parishes to encourage more face-to-face relationships— only 4 percent of Catholics believe either of these changes would hurt the Church.

Any effort to understand the way American Catholics feel about their church must give high priority to their attitudes toward the priesthood. The parish priest is the hub around which congregational activity revolves even as lay people play a larger and larger role in parish life. But church leaders have become increasingly concerned about the growing shortage of priests. The Hoge survey found that one Catholic in three— 34 percent—have personally experienced a shortage of parish priests. Given the fact that about one Catholic in five are not church members, this suggests that almost half of Catholics who are church members have experienced a priest shortage. Older Catholics, who are the most likely to attend church, have felt the shortage most: 43 percent of all Catholics over sixty have experienced such a shortage, compared to 37 percent of those age forty to fifty-nine and 31 percent of those under thirty-nine.

But only 32 percent of Catholics believe the solution to the priest shortage is to recruit many more priests; 54 percent believe the first priority should be to "think of new ways to structure parish leadership, to include more deacons, sisters, and lay persons." This feeling is considerably stronger among younger Catholics. Catholics over sixty favor recruiting more priests by 45–39 percent, while those under thirty-nine favor restructuring parish leadership by 62–25 percent. Women are also considerably more inclined to favor restructuring parish leadership; they favor that option two-to-one—58–28 percent—while men favor it by 50–36 percent.

	Total	<40	40–59	60+	M	F
FOR THE GOOD OF THE CHURCH TODAY WE MUST FIRST OF ALL RECRUIT MANY MORE PRIESTS TO OVERCOME THE EXISTING SHORTAGE IN PARISHES.	32	25	36	45	36	28

	Total	<40	40–59	60+	M	F
FOR THE GOOD OF THE CHURCH TODAY WE MUST FIRST OF ALL THINK OF NEW WAYS TO STRUCTURE PARISH LEADERSHIP, TO INCLUDE MORE DEACONS, SISTERS, AND LAY PERSONS.	54	62	52	39	50	58

Catholics are willing to accept some changes in order to deal with the priest shortage, but they strongly resist others. Changes deemed acceptable by at least half of Catholics are merging parishes (76 percent), reducing the number of masses each week (68 percent), having baptisms performed by lay deacons or lay officials (56 percent), and reducing the availability of the sacrament of penance and reconciliation (50 percent).

But there is overwhelming resistance to other possible changes: 74 percent say it is "not at all acceptable" to have no priest available for visiting the sick; 70 percent reject reducing the number of masses to fewer than one a week; 60 percent reject having marriages performed by lay deacons or officials, and 59 percent reject the idea of having only a lay administrator and not a resident priest in a parish.

CLERGY SHORTAGE—SOLUTIONS

	Very acceptable	Somewhat acceptable	Not at all acceptable
REDUCE THE NUMBER OF MASSES EACH WEEK	18	50	32
REDUCE THE NUMBER OF MASSES TO LESS THAN ONE A WEEK	6	23	70
BAPTISMS PERFORMED ONLY BY LAY DEACONS OR LAY OFFICIALS OF THE CHURCH	22	34	41
MARRIAGES PERFORMED ONLY BY LAY DEACONS OR LAY OFFICIALS OF THE CHURCH	14	24	60
REDUCE THE AVAILABILITY OF THE SACRAMENT OF PENANCE AND RECONCILIATION	13	37	45

	Very acceptable	*Somewhat acceptable*	*Not at all acceptable*
NO PRIEST AVAILABLE FOR VISITING THE SICK	6	19	74
NO RESIDENT PRIEST IN PARISH, ONLY A LAY ADMINISTRATOR AND VISITING PRIESTS	7	32	59
MERGER OF YOUR PARISH AND ANOTHER PARISH	25	51	21

While Catholics clearly like their priests and want them available at important times in their lives, they are very receptive to innovative proposals involving the priesthood:

■ 62 percent believe more recruitment of older men for the priesthood would help the Church, while only 10 percent believe it would hurt.

■ 48 percent believe it would help the Church to allow priests to resign their priesthood with an "honorable discharge" if they wish after ten or fifteen years of service; only 22 percent believe this would hurt the Church.

■ 47 percent believe it would help the Church to invite ex-priests who are married to become paid lay ministers; only 27 percent believe it would hurt.

■ 48 percent believe it would help the Church to invite married ex-priests to become active priests again; 31 percent say it would hurt. In fact, this proposal was less controversial than a proposal to allow priests to live where they want, not just in rectories: 35 percent said this would help the Church, and 34 percent said it would hurt. Catholics apparently don't care whether their priests are married or not—they just want them at the rectory.

In fact, support for a married priesthood is quite strong among Catholics, who believe by almost two-to-one—63–34 percent—that it would be a good thing if married men were allowed to be ordained as priests. There has been a steady increase in support for a married priesthood: 75 percent of Catholics say that if the Church were to change its laws and allow clergy to marry, they would be able to accept the change.

MARRIED PRIESTS

	Favor	Oppose
1971	53	36
1983	58	33
1985	63	34

Support for ordaining women lags behind support for a married clergy, but support for this change has also been increasing steadily, and Catholics are now evenly divided on the issue, with younger Catholics in favor of the change:

WOMEN PRIESTS

	Agree	Disagree
1974	29	65
1977	36	57
1985	47	47

While Catholics are divided on the question of ordaining women to the priesthood, they believe by 56–16 percent that opening up the office of permanent deacon to women would help, rather than hurt, the Church. In general, they favor a great increase in the number of permanent deacons by 64–3 percent.

Despite widespread concern about a vocations crisis, American Catholics still have great respect for priests and nuns. They reject by 80–16 percent the statement: "Becoming a priest is not a good vocation for young people anymore" and reject by 70–25 percent the statement: "It would make me unhappy if a daughter of mine became a nun."

There appears to be some conflict among Catholics about the role laity should play in church leadership. On one hand, they believe by 61–36 percent that "leadership in the Church should be restricted to bishops, priests, and deacons," and 36 percent believe that greater stress on priestly authority among the lay members would help the Church, with only 23 percent believing it would hurt. On the other hand, Catholics, by wide margins, support increased lay leadership:

▪ They support greater lay participation in parish decision making by 77–7 percent.

◼ They support more influential roles for women in parishes by 74–8 percent.

◼ They support allowing parishes to help choose the priests who come to serve them by 55–22 percent.

◼ They support full-time lay parish administrators by 55–17 percent.

◼ They support hiring full-time lay religious educators and liturgists by 67–8 percent.

◼ They support hiring lay marriage or personal counselors by 73–9 percent.

But there does seem to be a way to reconcile these apparent contradictions. Support for leadership by bishops, priests, and deacons and for greater obedience to priests indicates a respect for church leaders and a hierarchical structure within which lay people will exercise greater leadership. In other words, Catholics want more lay leadership within the Catholic Church; they do not want to change it into a Protestant church.

But Catholics do want and expect continued change in the Church. We asked a sample of Catholics what changes they expected to see in the Catholic Church in the United States over the next twenty years:

EXPECTED CHANGES IN THE CATHOLIC CHURCH IN THE U.S.A. IN THE NEXT TWENTY YEARS

MORE LIBERAL (GENERAL)	11
ORDINATION OF WOMEN PRIESTS	10
CHANGE (UNSPECIFIED)	7
LAITY MORE INVOLVED IN CHURCH DECISIONS	6
GREATER ACCEPTANCE OF DIVORCE	6
MORE LIBERAL ON BIRTH CONTROL	5
GROWTH	5
MORE CONCERN/HELP FOR OTHERS	4
ALLOW MARRIAGE OF PRIESTS	3
ATTITUDE ON ABORTION	3
MORE UNDERSTANDING/ACCEPTANCE OF PEOPLE	3
MISCELLANEOUS	14
NO CHANGES	12
DON'T KNOW	31

CONCLUSION

In some sense, these results offer no dramatic surprises; no more than 11 percent expect any one particular change. But if we look at the whole range of responses, an important conclusion does emerge: all of the expected changes cited often enough to be categorized were in the liberal direction: ordination of women and married men; changed attitudes on birth control, abortion, and divorce; greater lay participation; a general "liberal" change category. While 12 percent said there would be no changes over the next twenty years, these findings indicate that there is no expectation among American Catholics of a retrenchment—there is no expectation of a turning back on Vatican II. This is an important finding, because it shows that any Vatican effort to do so will meet widespread, if not almost unanimous, resistance among American Catholics. For the "People of God" in the American Catholic Church, there is no turning back.

V. A TOLERANT PEOPLE

One aspect of the Catholic "worldview" that asserts itself strongly again and again is a remarkable degree of tolerance toward racial and ethnic minorities, followers of other religions, and nontraditional sexual lifestyles. On a variety of measures, Catholics consistently show up as more tolerant than Protestants and, often, more tolerant than the general population. In general, Jews and those with no religious preference are the most tolerant Americans. But the differences we find between Catholics and Protestants are impressive because of their strength and consistency.

One traditional measure of tolerance has been attitudes toward interracial and interfaith marriage. Here, American Catholics are more likely than Protestants and, in many instances, the total population, to be tolerant. This pattern has held up for more than a decade and through a shift that has seen a dramatic increase in support for such marriages throughout the population. The most telling case involves interracial marriages. In a 1983 survey, Catholics evenly divided (47–46 percent) on the question of marriages between whites and nonwhites, while Protestants opposed by a 19-point margin (57–38 percent). Support among Catholics rose more than that of any other group in the population since 1978, when Catholics disapproved by 54–34 percent.

While strong majorities of both Catholics and Protestants approve of marriages between Jews and Christians, Catholic approval remains substantially higher. In the 1983 survey, Catholics approved by 86–6 percent, Protestants by 73–12 percent.

But there is a surprising gap between Catholics and Protestants on the issue of marriage between a Catholic and a Protestant; here, again, Catholics are considerably more tolerant. In the 1983 survey, Catholics approved of such marriages by 89–6 percent, an 83-point gap. Protestants, on the other hand, approved by 74–13 percent, a 61-point gap.

Another important measure of prejudice in American life has been a question about hypothetical candidates. For example, in 1958, Americans said by 53–38 percent that they would not vote for a generally well-qualified black man if he was nominated for the presidency by their political party; by 1983, the response had shifted to 77–16 percent saying they would vote for such a candidate. There is no difference between Catholic and Protestant response on this issue today, with 77 percent of each group saying they would vote for a qualified black presidential candidate. But two factors must be considered. First, the higher percentage of blacks among Protestants indicates that white Catholics are somewhat more supportive than are white Protestants. Second, Catholics were considerably more likely to say they would vote for a qualified black candidate throughout the years; in 1958, for example, Protestants by 58–33 percent said they would not vote for a black candidate, while Catholics were evenly divided, with 46 percent opposing and 45 percent favoring such a candidate.

Not surprisingly, 99 percent of Catholics say they would vote for a Catholic for President. The ratio for Protestants has risen to 89–7 percent, a considerable shift from 1958—only two years before the election of the first Catholic President—when 34 percent of Protestants said they would not vote for a Catholic presidential candidate.

Catholics are also slightly more likely to say they would vote for a Jewish presidential candidate, with 90 percent of Catholics and 86 percent of Protestants saying they would vote for such a candidate. Here, again, Catholics were more tolerant earlier: in 1958, Catholics supported a Jewish presidential candidate by 79–16 percent, Protestants by 55–34 percent.

Again, not surprisingly, Catholics are slightly more supportive of a woman presidential candidate, with 81–14 percent support, compared to 77–18 percent support among Protestants. Though the margin is small and support quite high—higher even than for a woman presidential candidate—Catholics are 6 to 9 points more likely than Protestants to say they would vote for a qualified woman mayor, governor, or congressional representative.

But the size of the gap between Catholics and Protestants is quite significant in two other hypothetical cases: voting for a homosexual or an atheist for President. Both groups oppose a homosexual candidate, but Catholic opposition is not as severe. Catholics oppose by 60–34 percent, a 26-point gap, while Protestants oppose by 70–23 percent, a 47-point gap.

The split is most dramatic, however, on the issue of voting for an atheist for President. Protestants, by 64–31 percent, offer a resounding "No." Catholics, on the other hand, say they would vote for a qualified atheist for President by 54–38 percent. These findings marked a continuation of two trends: increasing tolerance among Catholics and greater tolerance among Catholics than among Protestants:

VOTE FOR AN ATHEIST FOR PRESIDENT

	Catholic		Protestant		Total	
	Yes	No	Yes	No	Yes	No
1958	25	68	13	81	18	75
1978	47	46	30	63	40	53
1983	54	38	31	64	42	51

It was the Protestant reformer Martin Luther who said he would rather be ruled by "a smart Turk than a dumb Christian"; but in contemporary political practice, it is American Catholics who would rather be ruled by a smart atheist than a dumb believer.

In a 1982 survey, Catholics showed themselves to be more tolerant than Protestants, particularly Evangelicals, though less tolerant than those with no religious preference, in response to a question asking them to pick from a list of people they would *not* like to have for neighbors. There were no differences in some instances:

▪ 33 percent of Catholics, 31 percent of Protestants, 29 percent of Evangelicals, and 30 percent of the general population objected to having members of religious cults or sects as neighbors.

▪ 10 percent of Catholics, 10 percent of Protestants, 10 percent of Evangelicals, and 11 percent of the general population objected to having religious fundamentalists as neighbors.

▪ 3 percent of Catholics, 2 percent of Protestants, 2 percent of Evangelicals, and 2 percent of the general population objected to having Jews as neighbors.

▪ 2 percent of Protestants objected to Catholics as neighbors; 1 percent of Catholics objected to Protestants as neighbors.

Some differences appeared, however, in attitudes toward ethnic minorities, with Catholics being more accepting; the largest differences came between Catholics and Evangelicals:

▪ 18 percent of Catholics and 17 percent of mainline Protestants said they would not like Vietnamese refugees as neighbors, while the figure for Evangelicals was 23 percent.

▪ 22 percent of Catholics, 27 percent of mainline Protestants, and 34 percent of Evangelicals objected to Cuban refugees as neighbors.

▪ 16 percent of Catholics, 20 percent of mainline Protestants, and 25 percent of Evangelicals objected to Hispanics as neighbors.

The sharpest difference of all, however, came on the question of having unmarried people living together as neighbors: 14 percent of mainline Protestants and 32 percent of Evangelicals (more than objected to cults) objected to having these people as neighbors, while the figure for Catholics was 9 percent. Only 3 percent of those with no religious preference objected to having unmarried persons living together as neighbors. These findings reflect differences in attitudes toward the morality of premarital sex; as we saw earlier, a majority of Catholics see no moral problems with premarital sex, while Southern Baptists and other Evangelicals continue to regard it as immoral.

In another "neighbor"-type question going back to 1978, we found that white Catholics were more likely to attend an integrated church than are white Protestants: 60 percent of Catholics and 40 percent of Protestants said they attend integrated churches—even though only 3 percent of Catholics are black and the percentage of black Protestants is almost six times as high. Not only were white Catholics more likely than white Protestants to attend an integrated church, they were more likely to say they would like to have more blacks attend their church— 72 percent of Catholics and 62 percent of Protestants said they would like more blacks to attend their church.

In general, Catholics are more sensitive toward black concerns than are Protestants. For example, going back to 1965 and the height of the civil rights movement, Protestants opposed the involvement of clergy in civil rights demonstrations two-to-one, by 60–29 percent. At the same time, however, Catholics were evenly divided, opposing by only 44–40 percent. Similarly, while Protestants were split on the 1968 Fair Housing legislation, opposing by 41–39 percent, Catholics supported the bill by 46–30 percent.

Catholic sensitivity to minority concerns does not always translate into support for specific remedies: about eight in ten Catholics and seven in ten Protestants oppose busing school children for purposes of racial integration, for example. But the various attitudes toward blacks we have cited in this chapter establish sufficient ground to conclude that white Catholics are more likely than white Protestants to support minority concerns and causes.

One area where Catholics are considerably more tolerant than Protestants involves homosexuality. Catholics are more tolerant on a variety of questions. (Questions did not differentiate attitudes toward active and inactive homosexuals.)

■ According to a 1982 survey, while a majority of both Catholics and Protestants support equal job opportunities for gays, the Catholic margin of support is 43 points (67–24 percent); the Protestant margin, 31 points (59–28 percent).

■ In the same survey, Catholics rejected homosexuality as an alternative lifestyle by only 46–39 percent, compared to a 58–28 percent rejection by Protestants.

■ The 1982 survey showed that Catholics believe homosexuals can be good Christians or Jews by 67–23 percent, compared to only 44–40 percent among Protestants.

■ There is a significant gap between Catholics and Protestants on the question of whether homosexual relations between consenting adults should be legal. In a November 1985 survey, Catholics supported legalizing such relations by 51–40 percent, while Protestants opposed by 53–38 percent. This gap grew since 1982. One reason may be the impact of the spread of Acquired Immune Deficiency Syndrome (AIDS). While large percentages of both Catholics and Protestants said their attitudes toward homosexuals had been made more negative by AIDS, Protestants seemed to relate this change to attitudes toward legalization of homosexual relations, while Catholics did not; Protestant support for legalization dropped since 1982, while Catholic support edged up:

LEGALIZE HOMOSEXUAL RELATIONS BETWEEN
CONSENTING ADULTS

	Catholic		Protestant		Total	
	Yes	No	Yes	No	Yes	No
1977	44	41	38	48	43	43
1982	46	37	40	45	45	39
1985	51	40	38	53	44	47

Even in areas where a majority or a large plurality of Catholics oppose employing homosexuals, Catholics remain more tolerant. One sensitive area is the clergy:

HOMOSEXUALS AS CLERGY

	Catholic		Protestant	
	Yes	No	Yes	No
1977	39	49	31	59
1982	53	37	45	42
1985	46	48	36	59

The same pattern holds up in attitudes toward hiring homosexuals as elementary school teachers:

HOMOSEXUALS AS ELEMENTARY SCHOOL TEACHERS

	Catholic		Protestant	
	Yes	No	Yes	No
1977	28	64	23	70
1982	34	58	27	64
1985	41	53	31	66

In general, Catholic acceptance of homosexuality in society has increased in the past decade. There are a number of explanations for the high degree of tolerance among Catholics. One stems from the fact that Catholics are a minority themselves, and while they are certainly less aware of minority status than they once were, they are aware enough to be sensitive toward other minorities. The vast ethnic diversity and identification of American Catholics makes them sensitive to ethnic identification—including racial identification—on the part of others.

Tolerance *by* Catholics has increased alongside tolerance *of* Catholics. We have already seen the dramatic increase in the percentage of Americans who say they would vote for a Catholic President. Contact between Catholics and non-Catholics has also increased significantly: 67 percent of Americans say they have attended a Catholic religious service. A 1984 survey found that 77 percent of Americans say they have a favorable opinion of Catholics, who ranked third behind Methodists (80 percent positive) and Baptists (78 percent positive).

But, while cultural factors help explain Catholic tolerance toward racial and ethnic and religious minorities, they do not explain it completely. Part of the explanation appears to lie in the differing religious worldviews of Catholics and Protestants. This is most pointed in attitudes toward nonbelievers, homosexuals, and unwed couples living together. Protestants are more likely than Catholics to be offended by what they regard as sex-related sin—such as homosexuality or cohabitation or premarital sex—and less likely to support legal or social sanction for those activities. Catholics, on the other hand, tend to regard sexual activities as matters of privacy which do not necessarily have any bearing on the political or social order; Catholics do not look to the law to enforce sexual morality.

The Catholic worldview also asserts itself in attitudes toward other religions, as seen in the greater sensitivity toward Jews and the astonishing difference revealed in the fact that, unlike Protestants, a majority of Catholics would not be deterred from voting for a qualified presidential candidate who happened to be an atheist. A strong Catholic pragmatism is evident. Protestants, particularly Evangelicals, look first to find what candidates believe and then evaluate them from there; Catholics do not particularly care what people believe—they want to judge them on the basis of what they do.

CONCLUSION

One reason for greater tolerance among Catholics than among Evangelicals is higher education levels among Catholics, comparable to those of Protestants as a whole. Whatever the explanation of the greater degree of Catholic tolerance, the fact of that tolerance is unmistakable. Catholic tolerance of racial and religious minorities set standards to which American Protestants later rose. The conclusion is clear that American Catholics have contributed significantly to making America a more tolerant society.

VI. ECONOMICS

The U.S. Catholic bishops' pastoral letter on "Catholic Social Teaching and the U.S. Economy" has sparked the same kind of high-level national debate that their pastoral "The Challenge of Peace" sparked in 1982 and 1983. The leading critic is former Treasury Secretary William Simon; two Nobel Prize winners in economics, Lawrence Klein and James Tobin, have praised the document; members of Congress have held a hearing on it.

Economics has always been a key issue for American Catholics, who, for the most part, came to America as immigrants—fleeing the potato famine in Ireland, rural poverty in Italy, Communist persecution in Eastern Europe, and a variety of factors in France, Germany, and elsewhere. Like most immigrants, they brought little money with them and had to work hard to make ends meet. The late Monsignor Geno Baroni, a leader in labor, civil rights, and ethnic movements, used to tell the story his father, a coal miner, related about what he found when he came to America, where, he had been advised, the streets were paved with gold: "I learned three things. First, the streets were not paved with gold. Second, the streets were not paved. Third, I was expected to pave them."

As Catholics began paving the streets, working the mines, and manning the factories, they found themselves attracted to the labor union movement, which sought to organize workers so that they could bargain collectively with their employers for decent wages and working conditions. Labor's traditional appeal to American Catholics is easily enough understood: The unions played a major role in Americanizing new waves of Catholic immigrants, getting them decent jobs and incomes and helping them move up the economic ladder. Unions also have the Church's blessing: Popes have supported the right of labor to organize for more than a century, and Cardinal James Gibbons, of Baltimore, is a revered figure among union leaders for his support of the labor movement around the turn of the century. Unions also represent the kind of collective action favored by the Church.

The bishops' economic pastoral does not represent the first time the American hierarchy has addressed economic issues in a significant way. In 1919, as the nation began to resume life after the First World War, the bishops issued a program for "social reconstruction" that endorsed a number of proposals—social insurance, unemployment insurance— that later became part of the New Deal. The bishops' program for social reconstruction and the Church's identification with the labor movement combined to make Catholics a cornerstone of the New Deal coalition which turned government into an aggressive force for bringing justice into economic life. The New Deal philosophy fit into church teaching on the social role of the state. Since Pope Leo XIII's 1891 encyclical *Rerum Novarum (On Capital and Labor),* which dealt with problems created by the industrial revolution, the Church has emphasized the social nature of economic community and the responsibility of both individuals and government to work for economic justice.

There was one distinct difference between the pastoral letter and the 1919 statement: the first draft of the pastoral noted that the 1919 statement "emerged from, and was addressed to, a largely immigrant and working class community. Since then, the Catholic Church in the United States has become a multi-class community . . . as diverse in economic status and mobility as the general population of the country."

At this writing, the bishops have not yet completed action on their economics pastoral, so it is impossible to make a point-by-point comparison between their specific recommendations and Catholic public opinion. It is possible to say, however, that American Catholics are in substantial agreement with the bishops on broad economic themes: a strong role for government in economic matters, the role of circumstances in forcing people into poverty, and the need for tax reform and the redistribution of wealth and income in a more equitable fashion. On economic matters, the experience of the immigrant heritage and long ties with the labor movement have combined to reinforce church teaching. In political shorthand, Catholics have remained liberal on economic matters even though they have become entrenched in the middle class.

The transition between a largely working-class church and a largely middle-class church can be found in the stories of countless people working, saving, sacrificing, so that their children could have a better life; stories of skilled workers achieving some degree of financial security through the efforts of their unions; stories of young people who were the first generation in their family to go to college.

In terms of self-perception, American Catholics see themselves as slightly better off financially today than do American Protestants; they believe—by a slightly larger margin than do Protestants—that they are better off financially than they were when President Reagan took office. Catholics are also somewhat less likely than the rest of the population to report that they spend all or most of the time worrying whether their income will be enough to meet their families' expenses—16 percent of Catholics, 21 percent of Protestants, and 20 percent of the total population said they spent all their time worrying about finances, while 15 percent of all three groups said they worry most of the time.

But the fact that three in ten Catholics spend all or most of their time worrying about money is a clear indication that the new Catholic affluence is not total. So is another finding: there is no difference in the percentage of Catholics and others who report that there were times during the past year when they did not have enough money for food or clothing—one in five reported such shortages. Catholics were slightly more likely (24 percent) than Protestants (20 percent) to report lacking money for needed health care. These findings suggest that Catholics, like the rest of society, face the danger of a growing gap between an affluent middle class and a struggling working class.

One other financial note: Catholics also believe a family of four—husband, wife, and two children—needs more money than Protestants believe, to get by each week; this may reflect the higher concentration of Catholics in urban areas, where the cost of living is usually higher:

	Catholic	Protestant	Total
1982	$301	$278	$296
1983	301	292	296
1984	302	299	300
1985	323	301	302

Has the new Catholic affluence affected Catholic attitudes on economic issues? Some critics of the bishops assume that it does, that Catholics become more conservative on economic issues as they become more affluent. Let's look at some key questions raised by the bishops' economics pastoral and see how Catholic opinion stacks up against the bishops' positions.

The second draft of the new pastoral said: "The teachings of the Church insist that government has a moral function: protecting human rights and securing basic justice for all members of the commonwealth. Society as a whole and in all its diversity is responsible to build up the common good. But it is government's role to guarantee the minimum conditions that make this rich social activity possible, namely, human rights and justice. This obligation also falls on individual citizens as they choose their representatives and participate in shaping the public opinion.

"More specifically, it is the responsibility of all citizens, acting through their government, to assist and empower the poor, the disadvantaged, the handicapped and the unemployed. Government should assume a positive role in generating employment and establishing fair labor practices, in guaranteeing the provision and maintenance of the country's infrastructure, such as roads, bridges, harbors, public means of communication and transport. It should regulate trade and commerce in the interest of fairness. Government may levy the taxes necessary to meet these responsibilities, and citizens have a moral obligation to pay those taxes. The way society responds to the needs of the poor through its public policies is the litmus test of its justice or injustice."

The evidence is strong that Catholics have not abandoned their support of an activist government. Catholics have seen the positive impact of government in their own lives: they've seen their parents cared for by Social Security and Medicare; they've gone through college on student loans; they've worked in civil service jobs. The major area in which Catholic support for an activist government can be found is in support for increased spending for social programs. These results from a fall 1984 survey are typical in showing Catholic support for increased social spending above the national average. In the fall of 1984, for example, Catholic support for higher spending "for social programs like education and Medicare" was five points higher than that among Protestants. Catholics supported such increases by 77–22 percent, Protestants by 72–25 percent. The general population favored the increases by 74–24 percent.

Another survey taken approximately the same time shows slightly lower levels of support but the same pattern. This question did not mention examples of social spending, and it may well be that the lower

levels of support found indicate that support for social programs goes
up when they become more specific.

MORE GOVERNMENT SPENDING ON SOCIAL PROGRAMS

	Strongly favor	Favor	Oppose	Strongly oppose
CATHOLIC	22	44	20	5
BAPTIST	22	40	27	7
EVANGELICAL	17	40	27	8
PROTESTANT	17	38	32	7
METHODIST	14	39	36	8
SOUTHERN BAPTIST	9	40	40	8

The pattern of strong Catholic support for social spending is confirmed again in responses to a January 1985 question: 47 percent of
Catholics said the United States was spending too little on social programs, while only 17 percent said it was spending too much, a 30-point
gap. Protestants were only 13 percentage points more likely to say the
nation was not spending enough on social programs:

SOCIAL SPENDING

	Too much	About right	Too little
CATHOLIC	17	30	47
PROTESTANT	25	30	38
TOTAL	22	30	42

On a variety of social spending issues, Catholics are strong in their
support and often more supportive than are Protestants:

▪ In 1965, Catholics were more enthusiastic than Protestants in support of Medicare, backing it by 72–22 percent, while Protestant support
was 59–31 percent.

▪ In November 1966, a plurality of Catholics (49–34 percent) had a
favorable impression of Lyndon Johnson's "Great Society" programs,
while Protestants were strongly opposed (48–28 percent).

▪ Catholics are more likely than Protestants to support wage/price
controls. In 1978, Catholics supported reimposing wage/price controls
by 59–31 percent, Protestants by 51–35 percent.

■ Catholics are part of a massive national consensus in support of maintaining a cost-of-living adjustment for Social Security: Catholics, Protestants, and the total population each support COLAs by 88–10 percent.

■ Catholics support a program in which the government would provide vouchers to help the poor relocate near jobs by 56–33 percent, a 23-point gap; Protestants support such a plan by 49–43 percent, only a 6-point gap.

■ When it comes to deficit reduction, Catholics are more likely than Protestants to support cuts in defense spending and oppose cuts in social spending and entitlements; they are about as equally opposed to a tax increase, according to surveys taken in January 1985 and 1986:

DEFICIT-CUTTING MEASURES

		Catholic		Protestant		Total	
		Yes	No	Yes	No	Yes	No
CUT DEFENSE SPENDING	'85	68	25	62	31	66	28
	'86	63	29	55	37	59	33
CUT SOCIAL SPENDING	'85	39	56	40	53	39	55
	'86	40	54	46	47	42	51
CUT ENTITLEMENTS	'85	7	89	9	86	9	87
	'86	8	90	9	87	9	88
RAISE TAXES	'85	15	81	19	74	18	76
	'86	19	86	22	72	22	73

At the same time that Catholic support for social spending is high, so is Catholic support for fiscal discipline, as seen in support for a constitutional amendment to require a balanced federal budget and "line-item" veto power for the President. In 1983, 72 percent of Catholics and 66 percent of Protestants supported a balanced-budget amendment; in 1985, responding to a differently worded proposal, Catholics supported the concept by 45–30 percent, Protestants by 51–26 percent. In 1985, seven in ten Catholics and Protestants supported a line-item veto. In the context of all our findings, however, these positions do not undercut support for social spending.

While Catholics are more supportive of government social programs than most other Americans, they are no more likely to favor federal administration of those programs. In a 1981 survey, at the height of the debate over President Reagan's proposed "New Federalism," a transfer of key government programs to the states, 56 percent of Catholics, 56 percent of the general population, and 57 percent of Protestants favored concentration of power in state government. About seven in ten in all three groups said state governments were better able to understand people's needs and more efficient in administering social programs.

Catholics' respect for the role of government extends to government regulation in health and safety matters. This is a logical extension of their support for government social programs. For example, in a fall 1984 survey, 64 percent of Catholics opposed reducing pollution controls to cut business costs. This was only a few points higher than opposition among Protestants (61 percent); the interesting difference came with Evangelicals, who opposed reducing pollution controls by only 52–42 percent.

In the second draft of their pastoral letter on Catholic social teaching and the U.S. economy, the bishops criticized the growing inequality of the distribution of wealth in the United States. They said: "Catholic social teaching does not suggest that absolute equality in the distribution of income and wealth is required. Some degree of inequality is not only acceptable, but may be considered desirable for economic and social reasons. However, unequal distribution should be evaluated in terms of several moral principles we have enunciated: the priority of meeting the basic needs of the poor and the importance of increasing the level of participation by all members of society in the economic life of the nation."

Catholics agree with the bishops that income distribution in the United States should be more equitable than it is today, and are slightly more likely than Protestants to believe so. Catholics believe that money distribution should be more even by 61–28 percent, a 33-point gap; Protestants support more even distribution by 59–33 percent, a 26-point gap; the total population supports it by 60–31 percent, a 29-point gap.

One method of income redistribution supported by the bishops' pastoral is reform of the federal tax system. "Reforms in the tax system should be implemented that reduce the tax burden on the poor," the second draft said. "We urge that two principles be incorporated in any tax reforms that are undertaken. First, such payments should eliminate or offset the payment of taxes by those below the official poverty level. In recent years, the tax burden of the poor has increased substantially while those at the top of the income scale have enjoyed significant reductions. Families below the official poverty line are, by definition, without sufficient resources to purchase the basic necessities of life. They should not be forced to bear the additional burden of paying taxes. Secondly, we urge that the principle of progressivity be a central guiding norm in any reform of the tax system. Those with relatively greater financial resources should pay a higher rate of taxation—both in principle and in the actual or 'effective' tax rates paid. The inclusion of such a principle in tax policies is an important means of reducing the severe inequalities of income and wealth in the nation."

When President Reagan introduced his tax-reform proposal in early 1985, American Catholics were cautiously supportive, backing the plan by roughly the same, five-to-three, ratio as other Americans. Some reactions to particular features of the proposal are instructive:

■ 77 percent of Catholics, Protestants, and the general population favored raising more money from corporations and less from individuals.

■ Catholics were slightly less enthusiastic about dropping the top tax rate for individuals from 50 to 35 percent: Catholics supported the proposal by 48–40 percent, Protestants by 50–33 percent.

■ Catholics and Protestants were both evenly divided on allowing charitable deductions only for those who itemize their deductions.

■ Six in ten Catholics and Protestants opposed taxing employer-paid health insurance as income.

■ 54 percent of Catholics and 59 percent of Protestants opposed removing the current federal tax deduction for state and local taxes.

■ Catholics and Protestants held identical views that taxes for the poor would be lowered and taxes for middle-income families, big business, and small business would go up under the President's proposal. But there was an interesting difference in attitudes about the plan's impact on wealthy families: Catholics said, by 39–26 percent, that they would go down, while Protestants said, by 33–30 percent, that they would go up.

■ At first, Catholics and Protestants were both closely divided on the plan's impact on their own taxes: 32 percent of Catholics and 31 percent of Protestants said their taxes would go up, and 26 percent of both said their taxes would go down. Three months later, however, 49 percent of Catholics and 46 percent of Protestants said their taxes would go up, and only 10 percent in each group said they would go down.

■ Perhaps because of the different view of the plan's impact on wealthy families, Catholics and Protestants differed on the plan's over-

all fairness, with Catholics more likely to see the new plan as less fair
than the existing system:

		Fairer	Less fair	Stay the same
CATHOLIC	6/85	27	24	35
	9/85	21	23	45
PROTESTANT	6/85	31	19	35
	9/85	28	17	37
TOTAL	6/85	29	22	34
	9/85	25	20	40

These figures all suggest that there is general agreement between the
U.S. bishops and grass-roots Catholics on support for tax reform which
would lower taxes for poor and middle-income Americans and raise
them for wealthy individuals and corporations.

As far as poverty itself is concerned, about seven in ten Catholics and
Protestants believe poverty is increasing in America. But Catholics are
slightly less likely to view lack of individual effort as the sole cause of
poverty.

Catholics lean toward placing the major blame on circumstances,
over lack of effort, by 36–29 percent. Protestants lean toward blaming
lack of effort, by 36–33 percent; 31 percent of Catholics and 30 percent
of Protestants blamed both factors.

While Catholics are sympathetic to the victims of poverty, they are
also strongly supportive of the work ethic. In a 1978 survey, two thirds
supported a proposal to have welfare mothers register for full-time or
part-time jobs. In a 1985 survey, seven in ten Catholics and Protestants
supported a "workfare" proposal in which welfare recipients who could
not find jobs after finishing job-search and job-training programs would
be required to perform public service or nonprofit jobs without additional pay.

While the new Catholic affluence has not caused a callousness toward
the poor, it has contributed to a distancing of American Catholics from
the labor movement—despite the fact that 23 percent of Catholics live
in families with a member who belongs to a labor union and that 34
percent of all union members are Catholics. While Catholics remain
more supportive of unions than do Protestants, the gap is narrowing.
When Americans are asked their level of confidence in major institu-

tions in society, labor unions rank near the bottom. In May 1985, only 32 percent of Catholics and 27 percent of Protestants expressed a "great deal" or "quite a lot" of confidence in organized labor.

This is not the only indicator that American Catholics have significantly weakened their support for the labor movement. Both Catholics and Protestants now see big labor and big business as equal threats to the nation. Some 45 percent of Catholics and 52 percent of Protestants view big government as the greatest threat to the nation; 22 percent of Catholics and 21 percent of Protestants view big business as the greatest threat; 23 percent of Catholics and 19 percent of Protestants view big labor as the greatest threat.

Americans generally approve of labor unions by two to one. Catholics give unions a slightly higher approval rating, 61–26 percent, compared to 57–29 percent among Protestants. But Catholics and Protestants have the same low opinion of the level of ethics and honesty among labor union leaders: 44 percent of Catholics and 43 percent of Protestants rate them low or very low.

Catholics cannot be counted on to support labor's political goals. For example, 53 percent of Catholics and 52 percent of Protestants support a proposal to pay teenagers at a level below the normal minimum wage —a proposal strenuously opposed by labor. Labor's political clout is also low among Catholics. A May 1983 poll found that 30 percent of Catholics and 37 percent of Protestants said they would be less likely to vote for a presidential candidate endorsed by labor unions before the party primaries; only 18 percent of both groups said they would be more likely to vote for such a candidate.

The standard reason given for the declining influence of organized labor is that the people it once served have moved up the economic ladder and out to the suburbs and have less contact with unions. That is certainly the case with Catholics. But two noneconomic developments also play a role: labor leaders remained hawkish on the Vietnam War long after rank-and-file Catholics had turned against the war; this disrupted many old church-labor alliances. Finally, in recent years, Catholics have become part of a new American consensus which rejects "special interests"; while support for the concept of labor unions remains high, Catholics and other Americans tend to see labor leaders as one of a group of "special interests" putting parochial concerns ahead of the national interest.

The AFL-CIO has launched a campaign to give unions a more positive image and to strengthen their weakening position in American society. While Catholics are still more likely than Protestants to support the labor movement, unions have real reason to worry that they are losing their base of support within the Catholic community and should examine ways to revive their ties to American Catholics.

CONCLUSION

Despite a growing disenchantment with labor leaders, American Catholics are firmly committed to a strong role for government in economic matters—from pollution control to Medicare to antipoverty programs. Given a choice, they would spend more for butter and less for guns—and they would cut military spending before cutting social spending to reduce the national deficit. American Catholics remain and will continue to remain supporters of an idea rooted in both their faith and their experience: the belief that government must play a strong role in guaranteeing a healthy economic climate and meeting the needs of its people.

VII. DOVES FOR A GENERATION

From the time the U.S. bishops released the first draft of their pastoral letter on peace, in June 1982, they stood at the center of public debate on U.S. nuclear policy. The final version of "The Challenge of Peace," approved in May 1983, presented a stark challenge to existing U.S. and Soviet nuclear policy. It argued that while it was moral to possess nuclear weapons as a deterrent to their use, the bishops could see no actual use of those weapons that would be moral. The pastoral called for sharp reductions in nuclear stockpiles, a "halt" to the production, testing, and deployment of new nuclear weapons systems, and a rejection of first use of nuclear weapons. The bishops' deliberations guaranteed that it would no longer be possible to pretend that nuclear weapons did not pose a "moral" issue; their arguments were taken seriously by arms-control experts and may well have helped push the Reagan administration back to the negotiating table in Geneva.

The bishops also had their critics, and one charge leveled was that they were out of step with their own people. American Catholics, this argument went, were staunchly anti-Communist and were therefore "hawks." That argument was half right. American Catholics certainly are staunchly anti-Communist; they have no illusions about the nature of communism and they support President Reagan for taking a tough stand toward the Russians. But they are not hawks. In fact, they have been doves for a generation, and they show no signs of reversing that thrust.

For example, in 1981, Catholics believed by 53–42 percent that war is an outmoded institution; in contrast, Protestants were split, with 47 percent rejecting the concept that war was outmoded and 46 percent agreeing. Catholics were much closer to the total population, which saw war as outmoded by 50–43 percent. Another question in the same survey asked about support for a proposed United Nations resolution that would have banned nations from giving or selling arms to other nations; Catholics supported the proposal by a 22-point margin, 56–34 percent, while Protestants supported it by only a 9-point margin, 49–40 percent.

Catholics had a reputation as hawks from the days of the Cold War and the leadership of Pope Pius XII and leaders like Cardinal Francis Spellman of New York. And they clearly were hawks—more so than most Americans—in the early days of the Vietnam War. But Catholics turned very quickly against that war. It's worth taking the time to sketch the changes in Catholic attitudes toward the Vietnam War in order to understand their present attitudes toward war and peace.

In 1965, a small plurality of Catholics said they would be more likely to vote for a candidate who pledged to send a great many more troops to Vietnam; similar pluralities of Protestants and the total population said they would be less inclined to vote for such a candidate. By mid-1966, however, Catholics were evenly split, with 43 percent saying the United States should continue its presence in Vietnam and 41 percent saying it should withdraw; at this time, Protestants and the general population strongly supported a continued U.S. presence.

In July 1967, a plurality of Catholics for the first time disapproved of President Lyndon Johnson's handling of the war, though by a smaller margin than other Americans. Fifty-five percent of Catholics said it was not a mistake to get into Vietnam to begin with, but, by 52–36 percent, Catholics opposed Johnson's plans to send another 100,000 men to Vietnam—a larger margin than that among Protestants (47–42 percent) and the general population (49–40 percent). In November 1967, the U.S. bishops issued a statement saying that the Vietnam War met the Church's criteria for a "Just War"; at that point, they were moving in the direction opposite to that of their own people.

The now famous Tet Offensive began January 30, 1968; while the United States and the South Vietnamese technically won the bloody encounter, the cost was so high that it convinced many Americans that the war in Vietnam could not be won. Between February and March of that year, Americans shifted from describing themselves as hawks by a wide margin—52–35 percent—to an even split, with 42 percent describing themselves as doves and 41 percent describing themselves as hawks; Catholics followed the trend exactly. In April, 55 percent of Protestants, 56 percent of Catholics, and 56 percent of the population supported gradual withdrawal from Vietnam. When President Johnson announced that month that he would not run for reelection and that he was halting the bombing of Vietnam, 69 percent of Catholics, 64 percent of the total population and 61 percent of Protestants supported his decision on the bombing.

While American Catholics at first supported the war when it was "Johnson's war," by the time it was "Nixon's war," they had already rejected it and they continued to do so. In January 1969, as Nixon was inaugurated, Catholics supported a plan to "De-Americanize" the war by 51–38 percent, while Protestants opposed by 47–41 percent. By February 1969, 51 percent of Catholics said it had been a mistake to get involved in Vietnam. In June of that year, Catholics supported a ceasefire by 59–30 percent, compared to 51–35 percent for Protestants and 53–34 percent for the general population. Sixty-one percent of Catholics opposed immediate withdrawal, but, in a separate response, 61 percent also supported a phased, month-by-month withdrawal, and 47 percent said Nixon should proceed faster on withdrawal; only 16 percent said he should move more slowly.

In November 1969, Catholics described themselves as doves by 60–27 percent, while Protestants described themselves so by 53–32 percent. In January 1970, 58 percent of Catholics said it had been a mistake to get involved in Vietnam; in February, Catholics supported immediate withdrawal by 56–36 percent, Protestants by 57–33 percent. A dramatic split along religious lines developed when Nixon had U.S. troops invade Cambodia, in May 1970—Protestants supported the move by 54–29 percent, while Catholics were split, opposing by 47–44 percent. In January 1971, Catholics supported a plan to bring all American troops home by the end of the year by 80–16 percent, Protestants by 68–23 percent. In November 1971, the U.S. bishops concluded that Vietnam no longer met the "Just War" criteria—they had caught up with their people.

The last years of the Vietnam War also marked a major turning point in the way American Catholics viewed defense spending: they shifted from being more likely than other Americans to believe the United States was spending too little on defense to being more likely to say the country was spending too much. The best way to illustrate this is by looking at the "Too Much - Too Little Gap."

For example, in 1969 only 6 percent of American Catholics said the nation was spending too much on defense, while 56 percent said it was spending too little. Here, the "Too Much - Too Little Gap" was −50— larger than the gap for Protestants and the general population. The same pattern held up in 1972, when the TM-TL Gap was −33. But the pattern shifted by 1974: 46 percent of Catholics said the United States was spending too much on defense and only 10 percent said it was spending too little. While this reflected a national shift—a belief that the end of U.S. involvement in the war, in 1973, would lead to a "peace dividend"—Catholics for the first time were more likely than Protestants and the general population to say the United States was spending too much on defense.

That pattern has held up in every survey since 1974—on every occasion, Catholics were 1 to 6 points more likely than the general population to say "too much"; they were 4 to 12 points more likely than Protestants to answer "too much." For example, in early 1985, the total population said by 46–11 percent that too much was being spent on defense, a gap of 35 points. The Protestant TM-TL Gap was 33 points (44–11 percent). But the Catholic TM-TL Gap was 39 points (49–10 percent).

DEFENSE SPENDING

	Catholic		Protestant		Total	
	Too much	Too little	Too much	Too little	Too much	Too little
1969	6	56	9	48	8	52
1972	9	41	10	33	9	37
1974	46	10	40	12	44	12
1976	37	22	32	23	36	22
1977	28	26	18	28	23	27
1980	15	47	12	52	14	49
1981	15	50	14	53	15	51
1982	43	16	35	18	41	16
1983	46	11	41	16	45	14
1985	49	10	44	11	46	11

TOO MUCH - TOO LITTLE GAP

	Catholic	Protestant	Total
1969	− 50	− 39	− 44
1972	− 32	− 23	− 28
1974	+ 36	+ 28	+ 32
1976	+ 15	+ 9	+ 14

	Catholic	Protestant	Total
1977	+ 2	− 10	− 4
1980	− 32	− 40	− 35
1981	− 35	− 39	− 36
1982	+ 27	+ 17	+ 25
1983	+ 35	+ 25	+ 31
1985	+ 39	+ 33	+ 35

This pattern held even in 1980 and 1981, when about half of all Americans believed the nation was spending too little on defense. In general, the public thought the Carter administration was spending too little on defense, the Reagan administration too much; this may reflect more on perceptions about the two men's approach to military force than on the actual Pentagon budget.

The most dramatic shift came between early 1981 and early 1982. In 1981, before President Reagan's massive increase in military spending was passed, 50 percent of Catholics, 53 percent of Protestants, and 51 percent of all Americans said the nation was spending too little on defense; only 15 percent of Catholics, 14 percent of Protestants, and 15 percent of the total population said: "Too much."

But, a year later, after the arms buildup, the height of concern about Reagan's nuclear policies and the emergence of the nuclear freeze movement, 43 percent of Catholics, 35 percent of Protestants, and 41 percent of the total population said the nation was spending too much on the military; only 16, 18, and 16 percent, respectively, said "too little."

Other figures bear out the Catholic desire to cut defense spending. While all groups favor reducing the federal budget deficit by cutting defense spending, as opposed to cutting social or entitlement programs or raising taxes, Catholic support for such cuts is still higher than the average for Protestants. In 1985, 68 percent of Catholics, 62 percent of Protestants, and 66 percent of the general population supported cutting defense spending to reduce the deficit.

A survey taken in November 1984 asked Americans how they felt about increased spending for national defense. Here, again, Catholic opposition to increased military spending is the strongest:

MORE SPENDING FOR NATIONAL DEFENSE

	Oppose	Strongly oppose	Total oppose	Strongly favor	Favor	Total favor
CATHOLIC	41	14	(55)	10	27	(37)
SOUTHERN BAPTIST	38	5	(43)	11	39	(50)
PROTESTANT	35	11	(46)	11	35	(46)
METHODIST	34	12	(46)	13	38	(51)
EVANGELICAL	33	9	(42)	12	35	(47)

The shift in Catholic sentiment against the Vietnam War and the increase in Catholic dovishness on defense spending after the war's conclusion suggest that when commentators talk about "the lessons of Vietnam," it is Catholics, perhaps even more than other Americans, who have internalized those lessons. Why is this so? One explanation is that, to many Catholics, Vietnam was more "their" war than were other wars; it was supported as part of the Catholic crusade against communism; it was moved along by the first Catholic President; early on, it defended the ruling Diem family, which was Catholic. Other factors may well have come into play: Pope Paul VI made his dramatic appeal, "No more war! War never again!" at the United Nations in 1965. The American bishops' opposition to the war in 1971 was a major symbolic breakthrough, the first time they had opposed their government on a major foreign-policy issue. Pope Paul escalated his criticism of the war and in particular the 1972 "Christmas bombing" of North Vietnam. Catholic peace activists like the Berrigan brothers received national headlines.

But the Vietnam War caused a sea change among American Catholics. When it began, they were more hawkish than other Americans; when it ended, they were more dovish. And they have remained that way for a generation. That dovishness set the context for examining the impact of "The Challenge of Peace."

What impact did that pastoral letter have on American Catholics? Andrew Greeley has written about a National Opinion Research Center finding of a dramatic jump in the percentage of American Catholics who believed the nation was spending "too much" on the military between early 1983 and early 1984. Our figures do not find the same dramatic jump—perhaps because of differences in timing and wording of the questions. But they do show that the percentage saying "too much" has crept up steadily since 1982. Actually, the Protestant shift

(35 to 41 to 44 percent saying "too much" in '82, '83, and '85) is slightly greater than the Catholic shift (43, 46, 49 percent) in that period. In other words, Protestants are beginning to catch up with Catholics on dovishness.

Another way to put that, however, is that in 1982 and 1983—when the bishops were probably receiving the most publicity for their pastoral, even before it was a finished product—the Catholic TM-TL gap was 10 percentage points higher than the Protestant TM-TL gap. Though less dramatic than Greeley's findings, those figures support his contentions that 1) The bishops' involvement in the nuclear debate had a significant impact on Catholic public opinion and 2) that dovish American Catholics were ripe for the bishops' stand.

Some other findings also suggest that the bishops' peace pastoral has had an impact on their followers. A Gallup education survey taken in May 1983, just after the bishops approved the pastoral, found that Catholics were evenly divided on the question of whether a course on "the dangers of nuclear war" should be required for all high school students: 46 percent said it should be required, 45 percent said it should not. But a year later, 58 percent said such a course should be required and 38 percent opposed. In contrast to this dramatic shift, Protestants remained evenly divided in both surveys, supporting such a course by 45–41 percent in 1983 and 48–46 percent in 1984. There does not seem to be any development other than the pastoral that would account for a dramatic shift in attitude among Catholics but not among Protestants on this issue.

On a related issue, Catholic support for a verifiable bilateral nuclear freeze—extremely high to begin with—actually increased more than that of other Americans in 1984, even though the freeze movement itself had peaked by that time. In the fall of 1984, an incredible 84 percent of American Catholics supported the freeze.

	Catholics	Protestants	Total
11/82	72–20	71–19	71–19
3/83	70–23	67–22	70–21
10/84	84–14	76–21	78–18

Attitudes toward a nuclear freeze were much more intense than those about ratification of the SALT II treaty, signed by President Carter in 1979. The treaty was hotly debated throughout the country, and while sentiment shifted against the treaty, there was no difference between Catholic and Protestant views. Catholics moved from supporting ratification by 40–22 percent in June 1979, to an even split, 29–27 percent, eight months later; Protestants moved from 38–22 percent support to a 29–28 percent split.

It is not easy to say whether our perceptions shape our attitudes or our attitudes shape our perceptions. In either case, Catholics differ from other Americans in their perceptions of the relative nuclear strength of the United States and the Soviet Union: they are somewhat more likely than Protestants or the general population to perceive the United States as even or superior in nuclear strength. (See Appendix.)

Catholics are also more likely to see a continued arms buildup as a greater threat to peace than the United States falling behind the Russians in nuclear arms. (See Appendix.)

Catholic dovishness on defense spending does not automatically translate into opposition to specific weapons systems. On one hand, Catholics were considerably more likely than Protestants to support President Carter's decision to cancel development of the B-1 bomber; on the other hand, they were more likely to support President Reagan's decision to produce the neutron bomb. About half of both Catholics and Protestants support President Reagan's proposal to develop a "Star Wars" defense system, but Catholics are slightly less enthusiastic in their support; Protestants believe the program would make the world safer, by 51–31 percent, while Catholics hold that belief by a smaller, 48–36 percent, margin.

It is clear, however, that Catholic approval of President Reagan's handling of foreign policy, relations with the Soviet Union, and disarmament negotiations improved in direct proportion to a perceived softening of his foreign policy views, the resumption of arms control talks, and his summit meeting with Soviet Premier Gorbachev.

Reagan's approval among Catholics on foreign policy jumped from 39 percent in January 1984 to 51 percent in January 1986; support for relations with the Soviet Union jumped from 41 to 68 percent in the same period, while support for his handling of arms-control negotiations jumped from 49 to 61 percent.

REAGAN FOREIGN POLICY APPROVAL

	Catholic		Protestant	
	Approve	Disapprove	Approve	Disapprove
1/83	36	41	38	39
1/84	39	51	40	45
1/85	50	34	56	31
1/86	51	31	51	35

Relations with U.S.S.R.

1/83	41	39	43	33
1/85	53	31	57	29
1/86	68	19	65	22

Reagan on Disarmament Negotiations

11/83	49	35	48	35
1/85	52	33	53	31
1/86	61	26	56	27

The clearest impact of post-Vietnam Catholic dovishness can be found in attitudes toward Reagan administration policy in Central America. Catholic attitudes reflect both fear of turning Central America into another Southeast Asia and the pivotal role the Catholic Church is playing in the region. There are a number of American Catholic missionaries in Central America, and they are a new kind of post-Vatican II missionary, emphasizing social justice and community development, as well as preaching the Gospel and carrying out traditional works of charity. At the same time, bishops in the region have been outspoken champions of the poor and vocal critics of violence from both the Left and the Right.

For American Catholics, El Salvador conjures up two main images. The first is the assassination, in 1979, of Archbishop Óscar Romero, who was gunned down while saying Mass in the cathedral at San Salvador. The second is the grave containing the bodies of four American church women—Sisters Ita Ford, Maura Clarke, and Dorothy Kazel and lay worker Jean Donovan—who were murdered by right-wing death squads. All five deaths were the result of the Church's identification with the poor and their demands for social justice. Further militarization of the conflict in El Salvador is perceived among American Catholics as a threat to their fellow Catholics.

The U.S. bishops have made Central America a priority since 1979. A number of bishops have visited the area: Archbishops James Hickey, of Washington; John Quinn, of San Francisco; and Thomas Kelly, of Louisville, had to dodge bullets in the rioting that followed Archbishop Romero's funeral; in February 1985, a delegation of bishops met with government leaders in El Salvador and Nicaragua. Cardinal John O'Connor, of New York, outlined the bishops' position in congressional testimony stressing the regional nature of the conflict and the local conditions which created conflict, as well as the superpower rivalry in the region. "There is a temptation in this country," he said, "because of our justifiable concern about Soviet intrusion in the Americas, to ignore or misread the harsh realities that have brought revolution to Central America. Historic social inequities and historic repression, accentuated over the past two decades by economic advances that, ironically, deepened the disparity between prosperous minorities and impoverished majorities, were responsible for social unrest, which was then exploited by Marxist ideology. Masses of people, many of them awakened to a social consciousness by the teachings of the Catholic Church, have sought to assert their God-given rights to live in dignity and freedom."

The bishops support a regional diplomatic solution and oppose efforts to find a military solution. "The first requisite of a political and diplomatic solution," Cardinal O'Connor said, "is the recognition and acknowledgment that a military solution is neither possible nor desirable. To pursue a military solution, even while proclaiming the goals of political settlements, is to fail the test of political realism and of moral action." The U.S. bishops accept the need for sufficient military aid to keep the Salvadoran Government in power, but oppose significant increases above the 1983 level.

On most issues related to Central America, rank-and-file Catholics agree with their leaders; they have consistently been strongly opposed to Reagan-administration policy in the region. Our starkest finding came at the beginning of the Reagan administration and its efforts to find a military solution in Central America. American Protestants supported Reagan's handling of Central America by a wide margin, 56–19 percent. But American Catholics opposed his handling of the issue by 42–28 percent. Since then, there has been a major shift in opinion among American Protestants: Their opposition has increased to the point at which it is almost equal to that of Catholics, with about five people saying they disapprove of Reagan's handling for every three who approve. Now about seven in ten in both groups believe it is likely that Central America could become "another Vietnam"; Catholics and Protestants oppose increasing military aid to El Salvador three to one.

American Catholics also agree with their bishops in opposing U.S. military aid to the Contras in Nicaragua. "Direct military aid to any force attempting to overthrow a government with which we are not at war and with which we maintain diplomatic relations is illegal and, in our judgment, immoral, and therefore cannot merit our support," Cardinal O'Connor testified. "We are convinced that such military aid undercuts the possibilities of a political solution within Nicaragua and jeopardizes the political process elsewhere in the region. We believe that it violates existing treaty obligations and undermines the moral standing of the United States within the international community."

In early 1986, opposition to military aid to the Contras was greater among Catholics than among either Protestants or the general population. Nationally, 52 percent of Americans opposed military aid while 35 percent supported it and 2 percent supported humanitarian aid only. Protestants opposed military aid by 50–36 percent, a 14-point margin, but Catholics opposed by 56–35 percent, a 21-point margin.

Before turning from Central America, we should note a significant development in Catholic opinion on an issue no longer in the headlines: the treaties President Carter signed with Panama to return control of the Panama Canal to that country by the end of the century. When we surveyed the public in September 1977, Catholics were more opposed than Protestants to the treaties; but, four months later, while Protestant opposition had dipped slightly, Catholic opinion had produced a strong plurality in support of the treaties. This shift could well reflect the fairly visible position the U.S. bishops took in favor of the treaties. In September 1977, Catholics opposed the treaties by 52–34 percent and Protestants opposed by 53–45 percent. Four months later, Protestants continued to oppose the treaties (47–41 percent), while Catholics supported them by 49–37 percent.

THE UNITED NATIONS

In recent years, while Americans show no desire to withdraw from the United Nations, they have frequently been dissatisfied with its performance; more than half rate its performance as poor, and less than one third rate its performance as good. Catholics have been more likely than other Americans to say the UN has done a poor job. There is no obvious explanation for this difference. But the Vatican has long supported the concept of an international body to resolve conflicts, and it is possible that Catholics are quicker to criticize the UN because they have had higher hopes for it. But seven in ten Catholics and Protestants reject the idea that the United States should pull out of the UN.

THE MIDDLE EAST

American Catholics and Protestants sympathize with Israel over the Arabs by identical margins, 41–12 percent, according to a 1982 poll, which reflected a fairly consistent perspective. But there are two interesting differences. Catholics (48–20 percent) are more likely than Protestants (43–25 percent) to support a separate Palestinian state. This probably reflects a greater Catholic identification with ethnicity and nationalist ambitions; Catholics see no contradiction between support for a Palestinian state and support for Israel. A second difference can be found in reactions to Israel's invasion of Lebanon, in June 1982, in an effort to root out PLO bases. Catholic opposition (52–20 percent) was greater than that of Protestants (47–23 percent). One possible explanation here is the strong Evangelical support for Israel; Evangelicals, convinced of a special role for the State of Israel in God's plan for salvation, seem less critical of the Israeli Government's actions.

In the wake of the terrorist attack which killed 241 U.S. marines in Beirut, American Catholics were slightly more likely than Protestants to believe it was a mistake to send the Marines to Lebanon. A December 1983 survey found that Catholics said it was a mistake by 50–45 percent, while Protestants said it was not a mistake by 45–44 percent; overall, Americans believed by 47–44 percent that it was a mistake to send in the Marines.

Overall, neither Catholics nor Protestants give President Reagan very good marks for his handling of the Middle East. In early 1986, a time of relative quiet in the region, Reagan had only a 40 percent approval rating from Catholics and a 46 percent approval rating from Protestants for his handling of the Middle East, his highest rating so far. In January 1984, 61 percent of Catholics and 56 percent of Protestants disapproved of his handling of Lebanon.

SOUTH AFRICA

American Catholics are slightly more likely than American Protestants to sympathize with the black majority in South Africa over the white government there and to support greater U.S. pressure on the South African Government to end apartheid. Given the fact that 16 percent of Protestants and only 3 percent of Catholics in the United States are black, these figures indicate considerably more support among white Catholics than among white Protestants for South African blacks: In October 1985, Catholics sided with South African blacks against their government by 64–14 percent, Protestants by 60–13 percent. At the same time, Catholics supported greater U.S. pressure on South Africa by 49–16 percent, Protestants by 44–14 percent. Several factors may explain this difference. Catholic "dovishness" may be reflected in a greater willingness to pressure an ally to live up to human rights standards. Another factor is an apparent greater sensitivity to racial issues among Catholics than among Protestants.

BITBURG

An interesting difference between Catholics and Protestants emerged in reaction to the President's visit to a German cemetery at Bitburg, where it was discovered that SS officers were buried. The total population was evenly divided, with 42 percent approving the visit and 42 percent opposing. Protestants approved of the visit by 45–37 percent, while Catholics opposed by 45–40 percent. This may reflect greater Catholic sensitivity to the concerns of minorities, in this case Jews and other ethnic groups who opposed the visit because they believed it demeaned the memory of those who died in the war.

CONCLUSION

The breadth and depth of Catholic dovishness is one of our most important findings in this volume; the sea change in attitudes toward war and peace among Catholics triggered by the Vietnam War is one of the most significant public-opinion shifts in recent decades.

The new Catholic dovishness is not pacifism. Catholics still support a discreet use of force: six in ten supported the U.S. invasion of Grenada in 1983, and Catholics will support new weapons systems if they believe they will reduce the risk of war. But Catholic dovishness clearly goes beyond the Vietnam conflict itself. At one level, it translates into a commitment to avoid future Vietnams, as in strong Catholic opposition to Reagan-administration policy in Central America. At another level, the new Catholic dovishness translates into support for a lower priority for the military budget and strong support for arms control and reduction. On all of these issues, Protestants have to a considerable extent "caught up" with Catholic positions, moving Americans in general in a more dovish direction.

American Catholics, influenced by their church's leaders, their own experience with the Vietnam War, and security in their identity as Americans, are firm in their commitment to peace. They will be a major force for arms control, reduced military spending, and a prudent foreign policy for the foreseeable future.

VIII. THE SEAMLESS GARMENT

Abortion easily ranks as one of the most controversial social issues in American society. It involves matters of life and death, conflicting rights of the mother and the unborn child, as well as religious questions such as the definitions of life. The issue is particularly acute for Catholics because their church condemns all direct abortions, that is, procedures undertaken for the express purpose of ending a pregnancy. Catholic teaching does allow for indirect abortion, in which abortion is a secondary effect of a lifesaving procedure, such as removing a cancerous uterus or ending an ectopic pregnancy.

The issue was being fought out in the states when the U.S. Supreme Court, in January 1973, legalized most abortions in its controversial *Roe* and *Doe* decisions. The court held that a woman and her doctor could decide to end pregnancy any time within the first trimester and that the state had only limited power to restrict abortion beyond that, in the third trimester. The decisions were immediately controversial, and abortion opponents quickly began mobilizing to overturn them with a constitutional amendment, although, from the very beginning, the movement was not able to agree upon the wording of such an amendment.

The American Catholic bishops have made the abortion issue a top priority. Grass-roots Catholics certainly qualify as "pro-life" in their political orientation, but they are not a "single-issue" people. They also approve of legal abortion in a number of cases opposed by their church.

The bishops approved a "Pastoral Plan for Pro-Life Activities" in 1975 and updated the document in 1985. In "Pastoral Plan for Pro-Life Activities: A Reaffirmation," the bishops spoke strongly: "In fulfillment of our pastoral responsibilities, we the members of the National Conference of Catholic Bishops reaffirm that human life is a precious gift from

God; that each person who receives this gift has responsibilities toward God, toward self and toward others; and that society, through its laws and social institutions, must protect and sustain human life at every stage of its existence. These convictions grow out of our church's constant witness that 'life must be protected with the utmost care from the moment of conception.' In stating this principle, and in condemning abortion and infanticide as 'abominable crimes,' the Second Vatican Council restated a teaching which has been a constant part of the Christian message since the Apostolic Age."

"Abortion's direct attack on innocent human life," the bishops said, "is precisely the kind of violent act that can never be justified. Because victims of abortion are the most vulnerable and defenseless members of the human family, it is imperative that we, as Christians called to serve the least among us, give urgent attention and priority to this issue of justice. Our concern is intensified by the realization that a policy and practice allowing over one and a half million abortions annually cannot but diminish respect for life in other areas."

The "Pastoral Plan" calls for a three-part program:

1. "A public information and education effort to deepen understanding of the humanity of the unborn, the sanctity of human life, the moral evil of abortion, and the consistent efforts of the Church to witness on behalf of all human life.

2. "A pastoral effort addressed to the special needs of women with problems related to pregnancy, of men and women struggling to accept responsibility for their power to generate human life, and of all persons who have had or have taken part in an abortion.

3. "A public policy effort directed to ensuring effective legal protection for the right to life of the unborn," including "a constitutional amendment providing protection for the unborn child to the maximum degree possible."

In updating the "Pastoral Plan," the bishops incorporated the rhetoric of "a consistent ethic of life" enunciated by Cardinal Joseph Bernardin, of Chicago, chairman of the bishops' Ad Hoc Committee for Pro-Life Activities and chairman of the committee that drafted the bishops' peace pastoral. The "consistent ethic," also referred to by Bernardin as the "Seamless Garment," argues that the most effective strategy—and one that is truest to the Church's teaching—is to address abortion in the context of issues concerned with human life at all stages. On a practical level, this has meant linking abortion with the other public issues that have been a priority for the bishops in the 1980s: peace and the nuclear arms race, economic justice, and opposition to a military solution to tensions in Central America. Some right-to-life leaders have charged that this strategy effectively undermines the abortion issue by no longer treating it as a "single issue." Some bishops seem to share that view. But a solid majority of the bishops have endorsed the "Seamless Garment" approach.

The attitudes of American Catholics toward legal abortion are complex and often inconsistent. For example, 66 percent of Catholics believe life begins at conception, yet an identical percentage believe abortion should be legal in cases of pregnancy resulting from rape and incest. Starting with a clear-cut issue, we can see that Catholics reject "abortion on demand." Consider these findings from a 1984 survey showing that 65 percent of American Catholics reject the concept:

ABORTION ON DEMAND

	Oppose	Strongly oppose	Favor	Strongly favor
CATHOLIC	38	27	21	6
PROTESTANT	31	31	24	7
EVANGELICAL	29	55	7	4

These findings also reveal another pattern we will see repeated; there is often no significant difference on attitudes toward abortion between Catholics and Protestants, but this is because the figures for "Protestants" reflect the disparity of mainline Protestants, who are generally more supportive than Catholics of legal abortion, and Evangelicals, who are consistently even more opposed to legal abortion than are Catholics.

The Gallup Poll has asked an identically worded question on the Supreme Court's abortion decision a number of times since 1973. The question is as follows: "The U.S. Supreme Court has ruled that a woman may go to a doctor to end pregnancy at any time during the first three months. Do you favor or oppose this ruling?"

Some right-to-lifers have accused the Gallup Organization of bias in the wording of this question. They charge that it does not make clear that the court decisions allow abortion through the third trimester; they argue that that information would lead to a more negative judgment on the ruling. There is no doubt that it is impossible to summarize a lengthy, complex court ruling in all its nuances in one sentence, and

surveys we will look at shortly show clearly that support for abortion
declines in the second and third trimesters. But the question is an accurate summary of a key part of the court's decision and points to a period
of abortion on demand in the first trimester. Furthermore, the question
has been worded the same way every time it was asked; if it were going
to lead to a biased response, the bias would have been consistent.

Having said that, we can see that the pattern of responses to that
question has been fascinating:

	Catholic		Protestant		Total	
	Favor	Oppose	Favor	Oppose	Favor	Oppose
1974	32	61	48	41	47	44
1977	37	56	45	46	45	46
1983	47	48	50	42	50	43
1986	40	48	42	50	45	45

The trend shows a steady increase in support among Catholics for the
court's decisions—and then a decrease in support, although not an increase in opposition. The decline in Catholic support between 1983 and
January 1986 is less startling than the dramatic turnaround in attitudes
of American Protestants, who shifted from favoring to opposing the
decisions. There is no statistically significant difference between Catholics and Protestants on the question—indication of a merging of views
on the issue, as well as proof that abortion is not simply "a Catholic
issue." But there are important denominational differences among Protestants. The sample of Presbyterians and Episcopalians in the survey
was too small to be definitive, but it showed that more than 60 percent
in those groups favored the court decisions. Methodists also supported
them, while Lutherans were evenly divided and Baptists, particularly
Southern Baptists, opposed.

	Favor	Oppose
METHODIST	53	40
LUTHERAN	43	47
PROTESTANT	42	50
CATHOLIC	40	48
BAPTIST	35	56
SOUTHERN BAPTIST	30	61

A pattern similar to that found on the court decisions emerges in responses to another question asked over more than a decade: whether abortion should be legal under all circumstances, legal under some circumstances, or illegal under all circumstances.

The percentage of those saying abortion should be legal in some or all circumstances peaked in 1983, when 79 percent of Catholics and 82 percent of Protestants held that view. But there was a sharp downturn in early 1985, to 72 percent of Catholics and 75 percent of Protestants. While the percentage of Catholics saying abortion should be illegal in all circumstances returned to 1981 levels, it was still below the 1975 high point. But, while the differences are small, the 23 percent of Protestants saying abortion should be illegal in all circumstances in 1985 was the highest ever to choose that option.

It is difficult to explain the sudden switch. It has been argued that the media tended to favor the pro-choice position before 1985 and then began emphasizing the pro-life side of the debate; that would help explain the shift. The growing influence of the Evangelical movement may also be a factor. It is too soon to say whether this shift means opposition to the court's abortion decisions will return to 1974 levels, whether attitudes will stabilize, or whether this is a temporary aberration. But, at the very least, the assumption held by many—on both sides of the debate—that the public, including American Catholics, would steadily grow more accepting of legal abortion can no longer be taken for granted.

These trends make it clear that American Catholics are part of a broad consensus that opposes abortion on demand but believes that abortion should be legal in some circumstances. There is further agreement that those circumstances should include situations in which the mother's life is endangered and when pregnancy results from rape or incest. There is considerably more division in cases when the mother's physical or mental health is endangered or the baby will be born deformed. At the same time, there is overwhelming agreement that economic reasons are not sufficient to justify abortion.

Catholics have become more likely to support legal abortion to save the life of the mother at any stage of pregnancy. They have stayed about the same in attitudes toward abortion when the infant would be born deformed, and become less likely to support legal abortion in all other circumstances. Even so, in the first trimester, solid majorities of Catholics support legal abortion in the case of rape and incest, about half in

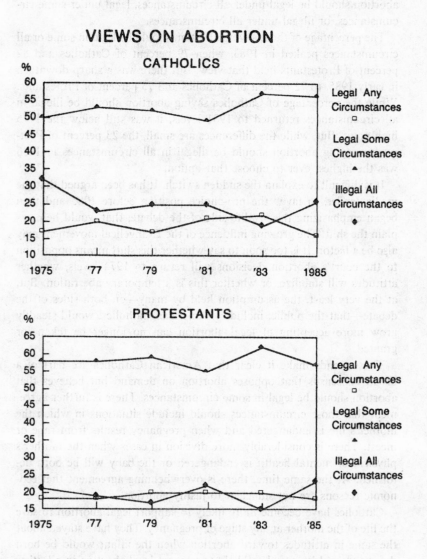

VIEWS ON ABORTION

CATHOLICS

the case of danger of physical harm to the mother, and about four in ten in the case of infant deformity.

LEGAL FIRST TRIMESTER

	Life of Mother	Rape/ Incest	Physical Health	Mental Health	Deformed Child	Cost
CATHOLIC						
1977	77	68	51	42	40	15
1979	82	57	46	39	41	15
PROTESTANT						
1977	77	63	54	44	41	15
1979	76	59	54	43	45	14
TOTAL						
1977	77	65	54	45	42	16
1979	78	59	52	42	44	15

LEGAL SECOND TRIMESTER

	Life of Mother	Rape/ Incest	Physical Health	Mental Health	Deformed Child	Cost
CATHOLIC						
1977	61	45	46	37	33	10
1979	62	28	43	29	35	7
PROTESTANT						
1977	65	36	45	38	29	8
1979	69	33	48	32	38	6
TOTAL						
1977	64	38	46	39	31	9
1979	66	32	46	31	37	6

LEGAL THIRD TRIMESTER

	Life of Mother	Rape/ Incest	Physical Health	Mental Health	Deformed Child	Cost
CATHOLIC						
1977	56	27	29	29	23	7
1979	63	17	34	19	21	4
PROTESTANT						
1977	60	23	34	26	24	5
1979	57	19	34	23	31	4
TOTAL						
1977	60	24	34	28	24	6
1979	59	19	33	22	28	4

In a 1976 survey, Catholics supported a constitutional amendment that would ban abortion except when the mother's life was endangered, by 52–42 percent. But, in 1984, Catholics supported an amendment that would also allow legal abortion in the case of rape and incest, by 59–38 percent. The 1984 survey illustrates the comparative Catholic and Protestant positions on abortion:

	Favor	Oppose
EVANGELICALS	66	30
SOUTHERN BAPTISTS	60	38
CATHOLIC	59	38
PROTESTANT	51	44
METHODISTS	44	53

We see again that Evangelicals are more strongly antiabortion than are Catholics and that the greatest gap is not between Catholics and Protestants (8 percentage points), but between Evangelicals and Methodists (22 points).

On another public policy issue, there is surprising agreement between Catholics and Protestants in opposing the use of public money for abortion: both oppose by 54–46 percent. Given different attitudes toward legal abortion itself, these figures suggest that some Protestants oppose using public money to pay for abortions they believe should be legal, and some Catholics support using public money to pay for abortions they believe should be illegal. This probably reflects greater Catholic support for government social spending in general.

But Catholics, like other Americans, have second thoughts about their position on legal abortion. A 1985 *Newsweek*-Gallup poll found that four in ten among Catholics, Protestants, and the general population answered, "Yes," to the question: "Do you ever wonder whether your own position on abortion is the right one or not?" At the same time, Catholics seem unsure about the best tactics to use to change the Supreme Court rulings. They split 42–42 percent in believing that "personally confronting and lecturing pregnant women entering abortion clinics" helps the antiabortion movement. Catholics strongly oppose disruption of abortion clinics (83–9 percent) and bombing abortion clinics (90–4 percent), showing no difference from Protestants on these points.

Catholics are somewhat more likely than Protestants to believe that "supporting or opposing political candidates solely on the basis of their position on abortion" helps the right-to-life movement, but they still see this tactic as hurting, rather than helping, the movement two to one: 54 percent say it hurts the movement, 28 percent say it helps. Protestants say it hurts by 56–20 percent.

Catholics are under no illusions that changing the law would have a dramatic impact on the number of abortions performed: 88 percent believe: "Many women would break the law by getting illegal abortions"; 81 percent believe: "Wealthy women would still be able to get abortions that are safe"; and 91 percent believe: "Many women would be physically harmed in abortions performed by unqualified people." Catholics also reject, two to one, the notion that "the moral tone of America would improve" if "abortions were made illegal under just about all circumstances."

Catholic leaders view abortion as one of a variety of related "life" issues. On these issues, there is even less difference between Protestants and Catholics and often a greater distance between grass-roots Catholics and their church's teachings. An important question involves the "right to die," a difficult question in an age when medical technology has made it possible to artificially prolong life long past the time it would expire on its own. Catholic teaching on this issue is clear, if not always understood. Father Edward Bryce, director of the Bishops' Committee for Pro-Life Activities, summed up that teaching in congressional testimony: "A patient is morally obligated to seek 'ordinary' treatment, that is, treatment which can be of real benefit and which is not excessively burdensome. One is not morally obligated, but is certainly permitted, to accept treatment which is complex, burdensome, and of uncertain benefit. Physicians generally have an obligation to supply the treatment a patient reasonably requests."

Several survey questions over the years have dealt with these issues. A 1975 survey found a surprising 37 percent of Catholics saying that a person had a right to end his own life if he is incurable, in clear disagreement with church teaching on such cases; 56 percent rejected the idea. Findings for Protestants were virtually identical. A 1985 question asked for reaction to a ruling in which the New Jersey Supreme Court upheld a law allowing all life-sustaining medical treatment to be withdrawn from a terminally ill patient if that is what the patient wants or what the patient's family and doctors believe he would want if he were able to make the decision. The general population supported the ruling by 81–13 percent, Protestants by 80–13 percent, and Catholics by 77–15 percent. There seems to be no conflict between this ruling and Catholic teaching.

A more controversial issue involves a situation in which a badly deformed infant who could live only a few years was born and the parents asked the doctors not to keep the baby alive. Catholics were more likely to disagree with the parents' decision, but the differences were surprisingly small: Catholics disagreed with the parents by 47–40 percent, while Protestants agreed by 43–38 percent and the general population by 43–40 percent.

Another important bioethical question involves *in vitro* fertilization, or what has publicly become known as "test-tube babies." It involves a procedure used to help women become pregnant when they are otherwise unable to conceive. An egg is removed from the woman, fertilized outside the body, and implanted in the womb for growth. Catholic teaching, which condemns artificial insemination, extends to this procedure, although when Louise Brown, the world's first "test-tube baby," was born, in 1978, Cardinal Albino Luciani, who later became Pope John Paul I, extended his congratulations to her parents. American Catholics were only slightly less enthusiastic than Protestants in approving of the new technique: 56 percent of Catholics and 60 percent of Protestants approved of the procedure. Fifty percent of Catholics and 53 percent of Protestants said they would use the procedure themselves.

One of our most startling findings concerns Catholic attitudes about surrogate motherhood, a practice in which a woman conceives a child through artificial insemination and carries it to term for another woman who cannot conceive. This practice violates Catholic moral teaching in two ways: One is the use of artificial insemination; the other is through carrying the pregnancy outside of marriage. While a plurality of Catholics—44 percent—disapproved of the practice, an amazing 39 percent approved of it. It was statistically identical to the 44–38 percent approval rating among Protestants. The total population approved by a narrow 42–39 percent.

A related, though not as exotic, issue involves the so-called "Squeal Rule," a Reagan administration proposal that would have required federally funded family planning clinics to notify parents when they provide prescription birth-control drugs and devices to females under eighteen. Given the Catholic Church's condemnation of artificial means of birth control, it might be expected that Catholics would be more likely than Protestants to support the proposal. But support was virtually identical: Catholics supported the "Squeal Rule" by 58–37 percent,

Protestants by 57–38 percent, suggesting that it was perceived as a "family" issue, rather than a "birth-control" issue.

All this information strongly suggests some basic conclusions about Catholic attitudes toward abortion. American Catholics are sensitive to the abortion issue and are, in political shorthand, "pro-life." But they are less than certain of their position and are reasonably tolerant of those who disagree with them and of legal abortion itself. It seems fair to conclude that the Catholic Church has instilled in its people a concern for the well-being of the unborn child which translates into a general rejection of abortion; but lay Catholics still have their own ideas about when that rejection of abortion may be overcome. Large percentages of American Catholics support legal abortions in instances—most notably in cases of rape and incest and a deformed fetus—which are condemned by their church.

Similarly, grass-roots Catholics, for the most part, do not see the connection church leaders see between the values involved in opposing abortion and those involved in such issues as *in vitro* fertilization and surrogate motherhood. There is more agreement with church leaders on such issues as care for handicapped newborns, but not as much as might be expected. It seems that the more likely Catholics are to see an issue as a matter of life, the more likely they are to agree with church teaching; but the more likely they are to see an issue as a matter of sex and familial privacy, as with *in vitro* fertilization and surrogate motherhood, the less likely they are to agree with the Church.

In terms of the style of debate about abortion, American Catholics seem much more likely to be influenced by the "Seamless Garment," rather than the "single-issue," approach. First, as we have seen, they believe, two to one, that single-issue politics hurts, rather than helps, the antiabortion movement. Second, Catholics do not give "moral" issues a high priority. In surveys about the most important problem facing the nation, economic and foreign-policy issues always rank the highest, while "moral decline in society" consistently ranks near the bottom. In fact, Catholics are less likely than Protestants to rank "moral decline" as the most important problem; over a ten-year period, as many as 4 percent of Catholics have cited "moral decline in society" as the most important issue facing the country only once; the average has been 2 percent. The percentage of Protestants citing "moral decline" as the most important issue rose as high as 9 percent and averaged 4.8 percent. (See Appendix.) A similar indication is that Catholics give a very low rating to the Moral Majority, which makes abortion a high priority. In

1984, Catholics disapproved of the Moral Majority by 37–26 percent, Protestants by 39–20 percent. (A high percentage of Americans were not familiar enough with the group to have an opinion.)

CONCLUSION

In the 1980s, the U.S. bishops have given highest priority to four issues: abortion, peace, Central America, and economic justice. They have strong support from their people on all four issues. For example:

- Six in ten support a constitutional amendment to restrict legal abortion.
- More than eight in ten support a verifiable bilateral nuclear freeze.
- About six in ten support cuts in military spending.
- Seven in ten believe Central America could become another Vietnam.
- More than seven in ten support increased federal spending on social programs.

It is likely, of course, that the percentage of American Catholics agreeing with the bishops in all four areas is somewhat lower than the percentage agreeing with any one. Even so, this still leaves room to suggest that a sizable amount of agreement remains. In sum, American Catholics are "pro-life," but they do not blindly follow their bishops on the issues and they are not single-issue voters; at the same time, they do seem to view life as a "Seamless Garment" and a value to be protected from the womb to the tomb.

IX. SOCIAL ISSUES

Part of the conventional political wisdom in America is that Catholics are "conservative on social issues." It is not uncommon for commentators to lump Catholics and Evangelicals together in this category. It is true that Catholics are conservative on some social issues, such as abortion. But they are quite liberal on others, far more so than are Evangelicals. And as we saw on abortion, even when Catholics and Evangelicals are in agreement, higher percentages of Evangelicals are likely to take the more conservative position.

The social issue on which Catholics stake out the most liberal position is women's rights. This has been a particularly controversial issue within the Catholic Church, because of the Church's ban on the ordination of women; many women have charged that this position makes the all-male church leadership insensitive on women's issues.

In general, however, the U.S. hierarchy has taken a progressive stand on women's rights. But that stand has been obscured by two things: First, the bishops' opposition to legal abortion places them at odds with the secular women's movement. Second, the bishops have sent out confusing signals on a top priority for the women's movement, passage of the Equal Rights Amendment to the Constitution. When the ERA was first passed by Congress, in 1972, the bishops took a position of neutrality. They argued that while they supported equal rights for women, they were concerned that the ERA would be used to provide support for a woman's right to abortion. Several dozen individual bishops supported the ERA on their own—just as some opposed it—but there was no official position.

Then, in the early '80s, a Pennsylvania court ruled that a state ERA mandated federal funding of abortion. After that decision, the bishops switched their corporate position and argued that an Equal Rights

Amendment without a clause stating that it was abortion-neutral was unacceptable. After further debate, the bishops in 1984 reverted to their original position of neutrality, while saying they would actively support an amended ERA.

But American Catholics seem oblivious to the bishops' wrangling over the ERA—they have made up their own minds independently, and they support it. The stereotype has emerged in American politics that those who are pro-choice are the strongest supporters of women's rights and that those who are pro-life are less supportive of women's rights. That stereotype does seem to hold up—among Protestants. Mainline Protestants are more pro-choice and more in favor of women's rights than are Evangelicals. But the stereotype does not hold up at all for Catholics: They are pro-life, but they are also strongly supportive of women's rights. They have consistently been 2 to 10 points more in favor of the ERA than have Protestants. The difference between Catholics and Evangelicals on this issue is even more striking: In 1984, 69 percent of Catholics and only 50 percent of Evangelicals supported the Equal Rights Amendment.

One interesting note: Catholics' beliefs about women's equality do seem to shape their views on related controversial issues. For example, on the controversial question of whether women should be drafted if a military draft is reinstated, Catholics support drafting women by 54–45 percent, Protestants by 49–47 percent.

We have already seen that Catholics are slightly more likely than Protestants to say they would vote for a woman for President, governor, mayor, or congressional representative. The same pattern holds up even on a question of near-unanimous agreement: In 1981, before President Reagan named Sandra Day O'Connor as the first woman to serve on the U.S. Supreme Court, Catholics supported the appointment of a woman to the court by 89–6 percent, Protestants by 84–9 percent. In a 1984 survey, Catholics agreed, by 32–10 percent, that the country would be governed better if more women held political office; the margin of agreement for Protestants was a more narrow 26–10 percent.

Catholics also showed more sensitivity toward women in a 1984 survey on the question of whether a male or a female President would be better suited to handle certain issues; even though Catholics gave the nod to a male President on five of six issues, they did so by smaller margins than did Protestants. (See Appendix.)

On these questions, Catholics are 5 to 15 points more likely to say that a woman would do a better job. This difference is most significant

ERA SUPPORT

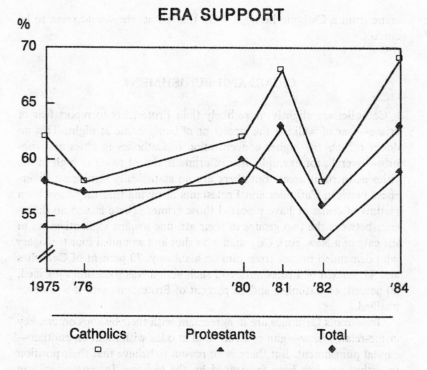

%

70

65

60

55

1975 '76   '80 '81 '82   '84

Catholics   Protestants   Total
   □   ▲   ◆

on the question of improving the quality of life for America. Catholics picked a female President by a 13-point margin, while Protestants were evenly split, picking a male President by 2 points.

One reason why Catholics are more supportive of women's rights is that they are more likely to believe that women still do not have equal job opportunity. For example, in a 1982 survey, Catholics rejected by 54–43 percent the notion that women now have equal opportunity, while Protestants disagreed by 49–45 percent. Another factor is the greater Catholic sensitivity to minority concerns. Finally, the internal debate over women's ordination may have served to raise consciousness of those on both sides of that debate about women's rights in society.

In early 1986, the president of the National Organization of Women, Eleanor Smeal, became involved in a controversy when a scheduled speech at the Catholic University of America was canceled because of her criticism of church teaching on abortion. Smeal, who was raised a Catholic, later spoke to a group of three hundred CU students off campus. She told the students that "a disproportionate number of feminists come from a Catholic heritage." On that point, she would seem to be correct.

CRIME AND PUNISHMENT

Catholics are slightly more likely than Protestants to report fear of crime—fear of walking the streets or of being home at night. This no doubt reflects the higher concentration of Catholics in cities and suburbs—overall, for example, fear of crime is almost twice as high in the cities as in rural areas. But there are no statistically significant differences between Catholics and Protestants in saying that they have been victims of crime or have reported those crimes. There is also no difference between the two groups in their attitude toward vigilantism, as in the case of a New York City man who shot and wounded four teenagers who demanded money from him on a subway: 70 percent of Catholics and 72 percent of Protestants said such action was sometimes justified; 20 percent of Catholics and 18 percent of Protestants said it was never justified.

Grass-roots Catholics are in agreement with their bishops on one key crime-related issue—gun control—and at odds with them on another—capital punishment. But there is no reason to believe that their position on either one has been influenced by the bishops. In particular, gun control has been a low-priority issue for the bishops, and there is no reason to believe that their position has influenced grass-roots Catholics.

Catholics are strongly in favor of gun control, particularly handgun control, and have been consistently more supportive of gun control than either Protestants or the population at large. In general, 73 percent of Catholics and only 52 percent of Protestants and 59 percent of the total population believe laws covering the sale of handguns should be stricter; 22 percent of Catholics and 37 percent of Protestants believe they should remain the same; only 2 percent of Catholics and 5 percent of Protestants believe they should be made less strict.

On the specific question of registering handguns, Catholics are somewhat more supportive of registration. Catholics support registration by 75–21 percent, Protestants by 67–27 percent.

But there is a major difference on the key question of a ban on the sale of handguns: Protestants are opposed to such a measure by almost two to one, while Catholics are evenly split:

BAN HANDGUN SALES

	Support	*Oppose*
CATHOLIC	49	47
PROTESTANT	33	62
TOTAL	40	56

Catholics are about 15 percent more likely than Protestants to believe that stricter handgun controls would reduce crime, accidental deaths, and deaths resulting from family arguments; for example, while Protestants believe tighter handgun laws would reduce gun-related family deaths by 49–48 percent, Catholics believe tighter laws would help by 64–34 percent. But the religious differences are sharper on the question of whether local communities should ban the sale of handguns: Catholics strongly support such laws (61–32 percent), while Protestants strongly oppose them (by 57–34 percent). Finally, belief is related to practice: only one Catholic in three reports actually owning a gun, while 51 percent of Protestants do.

Despite efforts by the nation's religious leaders, particularly the Catholic bishops, support for the death penalty in America is at its highest point in fifty years, and there is no difference between Catholics and the rest of the population on the issue: three in four in all groups support the death penalty for murder. Given a choice between execution and life imprisonment without possibility of parole as the penalty for murder, Catholics are slightly more likely to favor life imprisonment, although they still support the death penalty by 52–37 percent; Protestants support it by 57–33 percent, the total population by 56–34 percent. A slightly higher percentage of Catholics—25 percent, compared to 20 percent of Protestants and 21 percent of the general population—who support the death penalty say they would oppose it if new evidence proved it was not a deterrent to crime; of those who now oppose the death penalty, 18 percent of Catholics and the general population and 20 percent of Protestants say they would support the death penalty if new evidence proved that it was a deterrent. Similar majorities of both Catholics and Protestants believe that there is no racial bias in adminis-

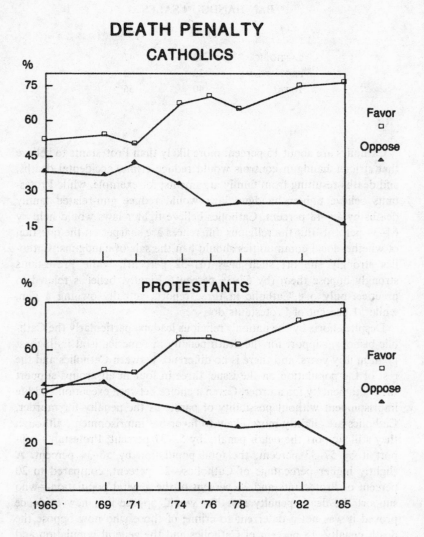

DEATH PENALTY
CATHOLICS

%

75

60

45

30

15

Favor
□

Oppose
▲

%
PROTESTANTS

80

60

40

20

Favor
□

Oppose
▲

1965   '69   '71   '74 '76 '78   '82   '85

tering the death penalty, but Protestants are more likely (65–30 percent) than Catholics (60–35 percent) to see economic bias.

Despite the popularity of the death penalty for murder, there is considerable reluctance to impose it for crimes less than murder.

	Catholics		Protestants		Total	
	Favor	Oppose	Favor	Oppose	Favor	Oppose
FOR ATTEMPTING TO ASSASSINATE THE PRESIDENT	55	39	58	36	57	37
FOR RAPE	46	44	45	45	45	45
FOR HIJACKING AN AIRPLANE	45	49	45	48	45	48
FOR SPYING DURING PEACETIME	45	50	50	46	48	47

For the most part, there are no significant differences between Catholics and Protestants in their views on prison reform: both prefer rehabilitation over punishment as the prison's goal, by two to one; both favor reforms such as literacy programs for prisoners, allowing prisoners' wives to visit them, and paying prisoners for their work, with a portion of their earnings going to their victims. But while both Catholics and Protestants say their states need more prisons, Protestants support more taxes to build new prisons by 53–41 percent, while Catholics oppose the higher taxes by 53–40 percent.

ALCOHOL, DRUGS, AND GAMBLING

There is no difference between Catholics and other Americans when it comes to smoking: four in ten Catholics, Protestants, and the total population smoke. But there are significant Catholic-Protestant differences in the use of alcoholic beverages and attitudes toward their regulation—Catholics are considerably more permissive. Several factors enter into consideration here. First, a number of Protestant denominations, particularly Baptists and Methodists, have strict rules against drinking; these denominations were the backbone of the Prohibition movement in America. Catholics, on the other hand, have never prohibited the use of alcohol and do not regard its use—as opposed to its abuse—as a sin. Moreover, Catholics place far greater emphasis on the use of wine in the sacrament of the Eucharist than do less liturgical religions. Second, alcohol is widely accepted among the ethnic traditions—Irish, Italian, German, French—which produce many Catholics. (Lutherans—coming from a more liturgical tradition, and particularly those with German roots—do not condemn alcohol and drink more often than do Baptists and Methodists.)

Catholics are more likely to drink and drink more often than either Protestants or the total population: four Catholics in five say they drink alcohol, compared to three Protestants in five (including only 45 percent of Baptists) and 67 percent of the total population; 72 percent of Catholics, compared to 65 percent of Protestants, say they have had a drink in the past week. Catholics are also more likely to drive after drinking: 52 percent, compared to 45 percent of Protestants, say they have driven after drinking, but the gap narrows when they are asked if they've driven when they have had too much to drink: one in five in both groups answers "Yes." Surprisingly, similar percentages of Catholics (31 percent) and Protestants (32 percent) who drink say that they sometimes drink too much; fifteen percent in both groups say they are trying to quit drinking.

Given the differences between Catholics and Protestants in attitudes toward drinking, there is surprising agreement when it comes to many proposed legal remedies: nine in ten in both groups favor tougher laws against drunk driving and a "Safe Rides" program: a confidential telephone network of high school students to provide a ride home for teenagers who have had too much to drink at parties; eight in ten favor a national law raising the drinking age to twenty-one; 76 percent of Catholics and 80 percent of Protestants favor mandatory two-day jail sentences for first-offense drunk drivers; four in ten favor random police spot checks for drunk drivers.

There are noteworthy differences on two proposals. Asked about a New Jersey Supreme Court decision upholding a law that says hosts can be sued for injuries caused by drivers to whom they have served alcohol, Protestants opposed by 62–31 percent, a 31-point gap, while Catholics opposed by 69–22 percent, a 47-point gap. Finally, 20 percent of Protestants and only 13 percent of Catholics favor a return to Prohibition—a law forbidding the sale of beer, wine, and liquor throughout the nation.

A final interesting difference between Catholics and Protestants concerning alcohol remains: While the differences are small, our surveys consistently show that Catholics are less likely than Protestants to report that alcohol has been a cause of problems in their families, particulary significant because drinking is more socially acceptable among Catholics. The difference has ranged from 1 percent to 6 percent in surveys taken since 1966. It may be that Protestants, with an inherently stricter view about alcohol, are more likely to brand occasional drinking a family problem. Whatever the case, Catholics are not immune from alcohol-related problems; the 20 percent reporting such problems is almost double the 11 percent reported in 1966.

MARIJUANA

There is no significant difference between Catholics and Protestants on the question of legalizing marijuana; both groups are strongly opposed to legalization.

But while Protestants extend their opposition to legalization of marijuana to decriminalization of possession of small amounts, Catholics do

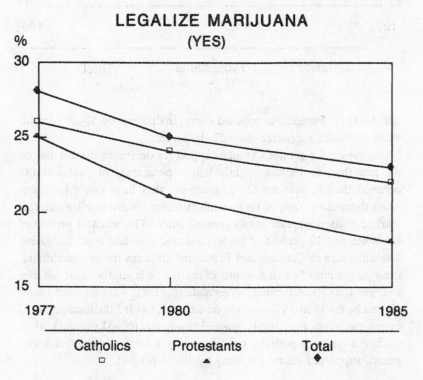

LEGALIZE MARIJUANA
(YES)

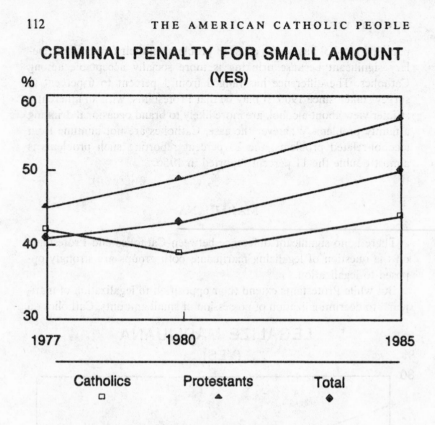

CRIMINAL PENALTY FOR SMALL AMOUNT
(YES)

not. In 1985, Protestants opposed decriminalization by 57–39 percent, while Catholics supported it by 52–44 percent.

One reason for greater Catholic support for decriminalization may be the fact that, in 1985, a slightly higher percentage of Catholics (33 percent) than Protestants (29 percent) say they have ever tried marijuana themselves. Despite toughening attitudes toward legalization, this marked a sharp increase in reported use since 1977, when 21 percent of Catholics and 19 percent of Protestants said they had used marijuana. The difference in Catholic and Protestant attitudes toward decriminalizing possession of small amounts of marijuana is another example of a stronger Catholic reluctance to legislate morality. Another such example can be found in a 1978 survey on attitudes toward the legalization of casino gambling. Protestants opposed two to one (60–31 percent), while Catholics, perhaps partially conditioned by a heritage of parish Bingo games, supported casino gambling by 49–40 percent.

SCHOOL PRAYER

Catholics are about as likely as Protestants to support school prayer, but they do so with less intensity. Opponents of school prayer, though still a minority, are making gains in both groups. In July 1983, Catholics supported a constitutional amendment to "restore voluntary prayer to the public schools" by 84–10 percent, Protestants by 84–11 percent. But in October 1984, Catholic support had dropped to 72–26 percent, Protestant support to 73–24 percent. The 1983 survey found that while 55 percent of Protestants supported the proposal "very strongly," only 41 percent of Catholics did so. At the same time, only 3 percent of Catholics and 2 percent of Protestants said the school was the most important place in a child's religious and spiritual development: eight in ten in both groups picked the home and the church as the most important.

Similar percentages of Catholics and Protestants—one in five—report that some form of prayer takes place in public schools in their communities: 14 percent of Catholics and 10 percent of Protestants report teachers leading silent prayer; 4 percent of Catholics and 7 percent of Protestants report teachers leading oral prayers; 2 percent in each group report teachers reading prayers.

PORNOGRAPHY

In a 1984 survey, similar percentages of Catholics and Protestants—eight in ten—supported tougher laws against pornography; but, in a pattern we have seen a number of times before, Catholic support was less intense than that among Protestants, particularly among Evangelicals.

TOUGHER PORNOGRAPHY LAWS

	Strongly favor	Favor	Oppose	Strongly oppose
EVANGELICAL	68	18	4	7
PROTESTANT	56	26	10	4
CATHOLIC	48	31	9	5

IMMIGRATION

One of the most controversial social issues of the 1980s is immigration. For decades, government leaders have warned that the U.S. economy cannot sustain an unlimited influx of illegal aliens coming into the country in search of jobs. At the same time, nothing has happened to stop that influx. Congress has tried several times to pass legislation that would help resolve the problem. One key feature is a ban on hiring illegal aliens and a penalty for employers who do so. The U.S. bishops, who have been active on immigration issues, oppose this provision; they argue that it would lead to discrimination in hiring against all Hispanics and anyone who "looks foreign"; but a large majority of Catholics, including Hispanics, support a ban on hiring illegal aliens, although the level of support has declined slightly since 1977. In 1985, Catholics supported a ban on hiring illegal aliens by 69–24 percent, Protestants by 80–16 percent.

The second key provision in the immigration bill is amnesty for illegals who have been in the United States for several years. The bishops support this proposal, but Catholics, again including Hispanics, reject it. In 1985, Catholics opposed amnesty by 52–39 percent, Protestants by 57–32 percent.

Given the strong immigrant heritage of American Catholics, the slight differences between Catholics and Protestants on issues concerning illegal aliens might be surprising. But a larger difference does exist on the question of immigration itself. A 1977 survey asked whether the level of legal immigration into the United States should be increased or decreased, or whether it was just about right. Among Catholics, 10 percent said it should be increased, 36 percent said it should be decreased, and 40 percent said it was just about right. Among Protestants, however, 7 percent said the immigration rate should be increased, 45 percent said it should be decreased, and 33 percent said it was just about right. American Catholics are still better disposed than Protestants toward new immigrants.

CONCLUSION

This survey, along with material from earlier chapters, shatters the stereotype of Catholics as "conservative on social issues." As we have seen, Catholics are "conservative" on some key social issues: abortion, the death penalty, school prayer, pornography, busing, and the legalization of marijuana. Even on these issues, however, they are less fervent than Evangelicals in their position.

At the same time, we have seen that Catholics clearly come down on the "liberal" side of other key social issues: most notably women's rights, gun control, civil rights for minorities and homosexuals, and the decriminalization of possession of small quantities of marijuana. In fact, the strong Catholic support for women's rights and minority rights is one of the most overlooked social phenomena in the nation today.

X. A PASSION FOR EDUCATION

I. CONSENSUS

Education is both a high priority and an emotional issue for Americans. Even those without children in school—or, indeed, even without children at all—recognize that education plays a major role in determining the quality of life in their communities and their nation's ability to perform in a competitive world economy. On a personal level, education affects our children; we want only the best for them in terms of academics and school-related social life. Education is also a sensitive issue, because it is the means by which we transmit values as well as skills. The fact that the public schools in the nineteenth century were overwhelmingly Protestant in atmosphere was the major reason immigrant Catholics formed their own school systems.

Given this context, then, the degree of consensus that exists between American Catholics and Protestants on public education today is truly remarkable: they agree in their evaluation of the public schools, their diagnosis of what ails them, and their proposed cures for those ills. While some fascinating differences remain, the amazing degree of agreement shows that education is an area in which a truly "American" consensus exists.

This consensus exists even though the percentage of Catholics with children attending private or parochial school is almost twice as high as that among Protestants, although, given the differences in the two groups' relative sizes, the actual numbers are probably very similar. A U.S. Catholic Conference study estimates that 28 percent of elementary-school-age Catholics and 16 percent of high-school-age Catholics are in parochial schools. Our figures reach a similar conclusion in a different way; the following chart from a 1985 survey shows parents' responses to questions about where their children attend school:

	Catholics	Protestants	Total U.S.A.
PARENTS WITH CHILDREN IN PUBLIC SCHOOLS	23%	28%	26%
PARENTS WITH CHILDREN IN NONPUBLIC SCHOOLS	9	5	6
NONPUBLIC/TOTAL SCHOOL RATIO	28	15	19

Despite this pattern, however, Catholics and Protestants have virtually identical views toward the public schools. For example, in 1983, the report of President Reagan's National Commission on Excellence in Education concluded that the quality of American public education was only fair and was not improving. While Catholics were slightly more likely to agree with the conclusion (by 79–11 percent), they were still very close in their view to Protestants, who agreed by 71–14 percent.

The report focused public attention on the public schools, and the schools' survey ratings improved significantly the next two years, when they were the highest in a decade. Catholics and Protestants give virtually identical grades to schools, teachers, and principals and administrators in their communities—and the closer Americans get to their schools, the better they think of them. So, for example, they rate their local schools higher than they rate the nation's schools; when parents with children in school are asked to grade the school their oldest child attends, the ratings go even higher. This consensus carries over in grades for teachers, principals and administrators, and parents of students in their communities.

For example, while only 27 percent of Catholics and 30 percent of Protestants give the nation's schools an "A" or a "B" grade, 76 percent of Catholics and 75 percent of Protestants give the school their oldest child attends an "A" or a "B" grade.

TEACHERS

	Catholics	Protestants	U.S.A.
IN LOCAL SCHOOLS			
A	13	13	13
B	35	40	37

	Catholics	Protestants	U.S.A.
C	25	25	26
D	6	7	7
F	3	3	3

IN SCHOOL YOUR OLDEST CHILD ATTENDS

A	22	27	25
B	50	44	46
C	18	18	19
D	3	5	4
F	2	2	2

PRINCIPALS AND ADMINISTRATORS

	Catholics	Protestants	U.S.A.

IN LOCAL SCHOOLS

A	14	15	14
B	33	36	34
C	26	23	25
D	10	10	9
F	4	4	4

IN SCHOOL YOUR OLDEST CHILD ATTENDS

A	22	30	26
B	48	40	44
C	18	16	18
D	5	3	4
F	3	4	4

Catholics and Protestants agree on the major problems facing the schools: lack of discipline, drug abuse, lack of proper financial support, poor curriculum and standards, and difficulty getting good teachers. Catholics and Protestants hold almost identical views in placing the major blame for lack of discipline in the schools on lack of discipline in home and in society. (Catholics are slightly less likely to say: "The courts have made school administrators so cautious they don't deal severely with student misbehavior" and to blame one-parent families for lack of discipline in the schools.)

Again, Catholics and Protestants hold identical views toward proposed solutions: six in ten favor classes for teachers on how to deal with problem children and discussion groups with parents of problem children; almost half support special classes or suspension for students with extreme behavior problems.

The Catholic-Protestant consensus on education carries over into the question of standards. Even on an issue on which there is no national agreement—the question of who shall decide what will be taught in local schools—the two groups think alike: About one fourth of both Catholics and Protestants believe parents should decide; one fourth believe school boards should decide; one fourth said state or federal governments should decide; and one in ten of both picked teachers.

When it comes to academic standards themselves, three in four Catholics and a like percentage of Protestants believe that promotion should be based on examinations. Similar percentages support giving students standardized tests so their achievement can be compared with that of other students across the country. Both Catholics and Protestants favor giving more homework to high school students, although the Catholic margin (52–26 percent) is higher than the Protestant (44–35 percent). When it comes to elementary school, Catholics support more homework by 43–35 percent, while Protestants oppose by a narrow 41–38 percent. About half of both groups oppose lengthening either the school day or the school year.

There is also consensus on the subjects that should be required for high school students, with mathematics, English, science, and history and government topping the lists. A consistent pattern shows that, for most subjects, Catholics are a few percentage points more likely than Protestants to favor requirements.

Both Catholics and Protestants show strong support for teaching sex education in high school, with Catholics actually showing a slightly higher level of support (80–17 percent) than Protestants (72–21 percent). These figures, from a 1985 survey, were virtually unchanged since 1977. At that time, there was no significant difference between Catholics and Protestants on the question of whether sex education courses should discuss birth control: Catholics, by 67–10 percent, and Protestants, by 68–5 percent, said that they should. The 1985 survey asked about sex education in elementary school. Here, the margin of support was smaller, but there was still no difference between Catholics and Protestants: Catholics supported sex education in elementary school by 54–42 percent, Protestants by 52–43 percent.

A solid 91 percent of both Catholics and Protestants believe that students involved in extracurricular activities should meet minimum academic and attendance standards. Interestingly enough, Catholics are more likely than Protestants to say that extracurricular activities are very important—by 44–37 percent.

About one in three Catholics and Protestants believe teachers' salaries are too low; fewer than 10 percent of each say they are too high. Catholics support merit pay for teachers by 61–23 percent, Protestants by 60–23 percent. There is also lopsided agreement that teachers must pass a regular competency test: Catholics support such a measure by 86–7 percent, Protestants by 90–6 percent.

While majorities of both groups oppose tax increases for public schools, there is no religious gap: Catholics oppose by 52–37 percent, Protestants by 52–39 percent. Again, given the lower percentage of Catholic students in public schools, the level of Catholic support for increased taxes to pay for public schools is surprising. While both groups support higher government spending for education, Catholic support is a little higher: 77 percent of Catholics and 72 percent of Protestants favored increased spending "for social programs such as education and Medicare."

On two specific funding questions, similar percentages of both Catholics and Protestants favor spending more public school funds on students with learning problems than on average students and oppose spending more on gifted than on average students. Their views are closer on additional help for those with learning problems: both support it five to four. Catholics, however, are more likely to also support extra funding for the gifted: 35 percent of Catholics and 27 percent of Protestants support such aid.

II. DIFFERENCES

While the consensus between Catholics and Protestants on education and public schools in America is astounding, several differences do remain. Not surprisingly, there is a major division between Catholics and Protestants on the subject of government aid to nonpublic schools. Catholics support a voucher system, in which the government would give parents an educational voucher to be used at the school of their choice, public or private, by 51–33 percent, while Protestants are evenly split, opposing by 43–42 percent. The overall public favors a voucher system by 45–40 percent. The general public is split more evenly on the question of "an amendment to the Constitution that would permit government financial aid to parochial schools": 45 percent support such a proposal, while 47 percent oppose it. Catholics back this proposed amendment by 67–29 percent, Protestants oppose it by 51–38 percent.

Catholics support tuition tax credits for parents of children in non-public schools by 65–31 percent, while Protestants oppose by 49–46 percent. This is an issue on which there is a sharp difference between Evangelical and mainline Protestants; for example, Evangelicals support tax credits by 53–40 percent, while most mainline denominations are sharply opposed. The increased Evangelical support for tuition tax credits reflects support for the Christian schools which have emerged in the past decade.

One significant factor is the views of blacks toward various proposals for providing government financial aid to church-run schools. While only 7 percent of blacks are Catholic, blacks support government aid to church-run schools: they support vouchers by 59–26 percent, a constitutional amendment by 55–32 percent, and tuition tax credits by 50–42 percent. This support seems to reflect significant black experience with inner-city Catholic schools with heavy minority enrollment—experience which, these figures suggest, has been positive.

Catholics are more likely than Protestants to believe that the increase in the number of private schools is a good idea:

	Good idea	Bad idea
CATHOLICS	64	18
PROTESTANTS	54	30
PUBLIC SCHOOL PARENTS	56	28
NONPUBLIC SCHOOL PARENTS	71	21
TOTAL	55	27

At the same time, Catholics and Protestants are equally likely to believe that the increase in "home schools"—parents teaching their children at home—is a bad idea:

	Good idea	Bad idea
CATHOLICS	14	75
PROTESTANTS	17	72
PUBLIC SCHOOL PARENTS	14	75
NONPUBLIC SCHOOL PARENTS	22	71
TOTAL	16	73

A near-unanimous nine in ten Catholics, Protestants, public school parents, and nonpublic school parents believe that private schools should meet the same teacher certification and accreditation requirements as the public schools. Only slightly lower percentages support the same standards for home schools. It is incontestable, then, that those who support private schools want those schools to meet the same standards as the public schools.

In addition to academic standards, parents who send their children to nonpublic schools are looking for discipline. Among public school parents, 25 percent cite lack of discipline as one of the biggest problems with public schools; among nonpublic school parents, the figure is 43 percent. By comparison, only 1 percent of public school parents and 2 percent of nonpublic school parents cite "moral standards" as a problem with public schools. While our surveys do not ask parents why they chose nonpublic schools, these findings suggest that they are looking for a disciplined atmosphere as much as—if not more than—they are looking for moral and religious values.

While different attitudes toward nonpublic schools are easily understandable, other, more subtle differences between Catholics and Protestants exist which are more fascinating precisely because of the degree of consensus. For example, Catholics are somewhat more likely than Protestants to approve of boys and girls playing on the same sports teams. These differences are small at the margins: large percentages agree that tennis and swimming should be co-ed and that football and wrestling should not; but, by equally slim margins, Catholics believe baseball should be co-ed and Protestants believe it should not. These findings really have nothing to do with education and are much more suggestive of attitudes toward sex.

Another difference concerns new uses for public school facilities. Catholics support the use of the public schools for tax-supported day-care programs for preschoolers by 51–35 percent, while Protestants oppose by 50–40 percent. Similarly, Catholics support the use of public schools for tax-supported afterschool programs for "latchkey" children by 48–41 percent, while Protestants oppose by the same margin. Again, these findings reflect educational concerns less than they reflect attitudes toward government social services—an area in which Catholics remain more supportive than do Protestants.

One educational difference between Catholics and Protestants seems to be that Catholics place a slightly higher value on education in general. Two thirds of both groups consider a college education very important, but other differences emerge. For example, we've already seen that Catholics are slightly more likely to believe particular courses should be required in high school; they are considerably more likely to favor more homework in both elementary and secondary schools; they are more likely to support spending additional funds on gifted students; they place higher value on extracurricular activities.

Some additional findings indicate that Catholics are more likely than Protestants to favor innovative courses on nontraditional subjects to give education a broader dimension. For example, Catholics are more likely to support public school courses on alcohol and drug abuse, parent training, computer training, race relations, communism and socialism, and the dangers of nuclear war and nuclear waste. (The more rural Protestants, on the other hand, are more likely to support driver-education courses.)

In several areas suggestive of academic intensification, Catholic expectations of future changes in public education are noticeably higher than Protestant expectations; this pattern suggests that Catholics expect, and perhaps look forward to, these changes: For example, 91 percent of Catholics and 83 percent of Protestants expect schools to provide computer access and training for all students; 74 percent of Catholics and 67 percent of Protestants expect more attention to teaching students how to think; 70 percent of Catholics and 65 percent of Protestants expect the first two years of college to be covered in high school; 60 percent of Catholics and 48 percent of Protestants expect more attention to individual instruction.

The strong Catholic emphasis on education includes a strong emphasis on science; in fact, it seems that Catholics are more interested in science than are Protestants. For example, they are more likely to support courses in computer training and to expect an emphasis on such courses in the future. Significantly, Catholics support higher pay for mathematics and science teachers to attract teachers to these key fields by a wider margin than do Protestants: 53–33 percent, as opposed to 47–37 percent.

These attitudes toward science are reflected in a 1982 survey which asked Americans whether they were more or less likely to believe that science can answer the problems of the world as compared to five years before. Catholics were considerably more likely to say "More likely." Forty-eight percent of Catholics and 29 percent of Protestants say they are more likely to believe that science can provide answers than they were five years ago; 37 percent of Catholics and 53 percent of Protestants said they were less likely to do so. Another question asked whether they were more likely to think that religion can answer the problems of the world as compared to five years ago: 48 percent of Catholics and 63 percent of Protestants said they were more likely to believe it could; 27 percent of Catholics and 19 percent of Protestants said they were less likely to hold that belief.

These findings strongly suggest that Catholics are more likely than Protestants to see science as compatible with their faith. There are several possible reasons for this. First, the findings reflect a strong Evangelical presence among Protestants, which is often suspect of science—as in the conflict many Evangelicals see between evolution and the biblical account of Creation. Catholics, on the other hand, have been taught that there need be no such conflict as long as they believe that the creative hand of God guided the evolutionary process.

Despite the history of the Catholic Church's condemnation of Galileo, who argued that the earth revolved around the sun, the Church has taught that science and religion can be compatible. In recent years, Pope John Paul II has addressed scientists on a number of occasions: In 1982, he sent delegations from the Pontifical Academy of Science to meet with world leaders to warn them of the disastrous medical consequences of nuclear war. Astronomer Carl Sagan, author of *Cosmos*, says that, under Pope John Paul's leadership, there had been "a dramatic increase in dialogue between the Catholic Church and science."

These findings suggest that Catholics are highly concerned about science and technology. One clear implication of this is that Catholic educational institutions will face pressure to provide adequate training in these areas. A recent study conducted for the National Catholic Education Association by The Search Institute, in Minneapolis, found that students who enter Catholic high schools after attending Catholic elementary schools are at a considerable disadvantage in science to those who enter from public schools. Catholic schools that do not keep up in science and technology face weakened support in the future.

CONCLUSION

When it comes to education, Catholics are like other Americans— only more so. They want quality education for their children and for everyone's children—and whether it takes place in a public or a parochial school does not seem to matter all that much. Catholics seem satisfied with the parochial schools that exist, but their reluctance to pay additional taxes for public schools and the increased Catholic shift to the suburbs, where discipline is less of a problem than it is in the inner city, suggest that long-term Catholic support for a network of suburban parochial schools cannot be taken for granted.

In fact, a major conclusion to be drawn from our data is that American Catholics are far more supportive of the public schools than anyone —certainly the Church's leadership—previously believed: They rate them high and want government to spend more money on them; a sizable minority are even willing to pay higher taxes for them—even though they are less likely than other Americans to have children in public schools. The combination of high support for both tuition tax credits and government educational programs indicates that American Catholics do not see an "either-or" situation—they want to help all schools maintain high academic standards.

But there is a serious split between American Catholics and their leaders over education. Lay Catholics support both parochial and public school systems: They put into practice the Catholic school community's rhetoric about a "partnership" between public and nonpublic schools. Catholics are highly visible on school boards and public school staffs across the country. But, at the institutional level, Catholic organizations function almost exclusively as special-interest lobbies for Catholic schools. They have a right and a duty to support Catholic schools— but if they continue to appear solely as parochial school lobbyists, they run the risk of alienating three out of four Catholic parents with children in public schools and a broader base of Catholics concerned with education as a general issue.

There are some hopeful signs that Catholic leaders are coming to appreciate the need to address public education. Throughout the '80s, the U.S. Catholic Conference has fought budget cuts in federal education programs. The bishops have asked the USCC education committee to develop a statement on values in public education. And several bishops commenting on the second draft of the pastoral letter on economics emphasized the role of education, both public and private, in combating poverty.

The "split" between Catholic leadership and lay Catholics over education can be formulated in a more positive light: a real opportunity exists for Catholic leaders to tap into strong grass-roots support in a campaign to improve the quality of education at all levels and in all schools.

XI. POLITICS

The political behavior of American Catholics is a matter of vital importance to both political parties; while Catholics once joked that their Democratic Party registration cards came along with their baptismal certificates, there has been a major shift toward the Republican Party, particularly at the presidential level, in the 1980s. While a plurality of Catholics still identify themselves as Democrats and at least 55 percent can be counted on to vote for Democratic congressional candidates, Catholics are now more than ever a two-party denomination. The geographical concentration of Catholics is also important: They make up 26 percent of the population in the Midwest and the West and a full 44 percent of the population in the East.

Catholics have been a key, though often unappreciated, element of the Democratic Party since the mid-nineteenth century. The Democrats wooed the massive influx of immigrants who came into the cities, providing human services at the precinct level at the same time the Republican Party was the home of the Know-Nothing Movement, of nativist anti-Catholics. The Catholic ties to the party were reinforced by the growth of the labor movement, which organized new immigrants and found its political home with the Democrats. Franklin Roosevelt's New Deal legislation closely paralleled the U.S. Catholic bishops' 1919 program of reconstruction, which called for programs such as social security and unemployment insurance.

In 1928, the Democrats became the first party to nominate a Catholic —New York governor Al Smith—for the presidency. Smith lost after suffering anti-Catholic bias throughout the campaign. But he drew 85–90 percent of the vote of Catholics and others in urban areas, setting the stage for Roosevelt's New Deal coalition. In 1932, Catholics voted for Roosevelt in about the same percentage they had voted for Smith, dropping off to about 73 percent in FDR's last two elections. Sixty-six percent voted for Harry Truman in the 1948 three-man race.

Dwight D. Eisenhower's landslide victories in 1952 and 1956 showed that the Democratic stranglehold on Catholic votes had weakened. The popular World War II hero held Democrat Adlai Stevenson to 56 percent of the Catholic vote in 1952 and 51 percent in 1956. In 1960, the Democrats nominated another Catholic, the young Massachusetts senator John F. Kennedy. A speech to Protestant ministers in Houston declaring his support for the separation of church and state reassured enough Protestants to keep the South in the Democratic column, and Kennedy's 78 percent of the Catholic vote solidified the North and the Midwest. In 1964, after Kennedy's assassination, Lyndon Johnson pulled 73 percent of the Catholic vote in his sweep of Barry Goldwater.

Hubert Humphrey—whose running mate, Edmund Muskie, was a Catholic—outpolled Richard Nixon by 59–33 percent among Catholics in 1968, with 8 percent voting for third-party candidate George Wallace, but Nixon won a tight race with only 43 percent of the total vote.

The largest Catholic defection since Stevenson occurred in 1972, when Catholics voted for Nixon by 52–48 percent over George McGovern, who was viewed by many as too radical to be President. McGovern picked a popular Catholic senator, Thomas Eagleton of Missouri, as his running mate, but dropped him from the ticket after his past mental problems were revealed—a move that could well have alienated some Catholic support, even though McGovern's final running mate, former Peace Corps and Office of Economic Opportunity director Sargent Shriver, was also a Catholic.

But Catholic support for Nixon cooled during his second term as the details of the Watergate scandal became public. In fact, a major split between Catholics and Protestants developed over Nixon. In January 1974, Protestants were opposed to Nixon's resigning by 53–40 percent, while Catholics favored his resignation by 56–37 percent. And while Protestants, the same month, opposed Nixon's impeachment by 59–31 percent, Catholics were evenly split, opposing by only 46–44 percent. By May, a plurality of Protestants—43–37 percent—had come to favor impeachment, while Catholics supported impeachment by almost two to one, 56–29 percent. When Nixon resigned in August 1974, he had a 60 percent disapproval rating among Protestants and a 73 percent disapproval rating among Catholics.

When Gerald Ford became President, after Nixon's resignation, Catholics followed the same pattern as the general population, expressing strong support at first, then dropping off substantially after Ford pardoned Nixon for Watergate-related offenses. Even so, Catholics remained slightly less supportive of Ford than did Protestants; at his low point, for example, only 36 percent of Catholics and 41 percent of Protestants approved of his performance in office.

Ford's Democratic opponent in 1976 was former Georgia governor Jimmy Carter, a Southern Baptist Sunday school teacher. There was considerable talk during the campaign about Carter's "Catholic problem." In fact, there were two distinct Catholic problems. One was concern about how well Catholics would take to a Southern Baptist in light of the kind of anti-Catholicism associated with the South in Al Smith's day and later. The second problem was Carter's clash with the U.S. Catholic bishops over the abortion issue; though Carter agreed with the bishops in opposing federal funding for abortion, he disagreed with them in opposing a constitutional amendment to overturn the Supreme Court's 1973 decisions legalizing most abortions. Statements by the bishops that they were "disappointed" by Carter's stand and "encouraged" by President Ford's support for a states' rights amendment created the impression that the bishops were endorsing Ford; the bishops put out a statement reaffirming their neutrality and advising Catholics to study a wide range of issues and to vote their consciences. Carter picked as his running mate Minnesota senator Walter Mondale, a protégé of Hubert Humphrey, the 1968 candidate who had been popular with Catholics.

A Gallup survey taken on the eve of the election asked Americans whether Carter's born-again religion made them more or less likely to vote against him. Despite concern about Carter's "Catholic" problem, only 7 percent of Catholics said they were less likely to vote for Carter because of his religion, while 9 percent said they were more likely to vote for Carter because of his religion. Protestants said, by 24–6 percent, that they were more likely to vote for Carter because of his religion, and he ended up with 46 percent of the Protestant vote, second only to Lyndon Johnson's 55 percent in 1964 among Democrats in elections since 1952. Catholics returned to the Democratic Party, voting for Carter by 57–42 percent over Ford, with less than 1 percent voting for independent candidate Eugene McCarthy (a Catholic).

Carter began his term in office with a strong vote of support from Catholics, who gave him a 74 percent approval rating, compared to 71 percent among Protestants. But as Carter's popularity declined among the general population, he lost even greater support from Catholics; in

August 1980, Catholics disapproved of his performance in office by 58–31 percent, a 27-point gap, while Protestants disapproved by 52–35 percent, a 17-point gap.

In 1980, the final preelection Gallup Poll found 47 percent of Catholics supporting the Republican candidate, former California governor Ronald Reagan; 46 percent supporting Carter; and 6 percent supporting independent candidate John Anderson. Election Day exit polls found that Reagan had received about 51 percent of the Catholic vote, Carter 40 percent, and Anderson 9 percent. This is the only recent election in which Catholics did not vote more heavily Democratic on Election Day than was indicated by late polls; the reason is the last-minute national drift away from Carter when a deal to free U.S. hostages in Iran fell through the weekend before the election. The other key factors appeared to be general dissatisfaction with Carter over the economy and an empathy with Reagan, whose father was a Catholic. While Reagan's Catholic vote in 1980 was no higher than Eisenhower's or Nixon's in 1972, it represented a historic 11-point lead over the Democratic candidate because of the votes that went to Anderson. But a majority of Catholics voted for Democratic congressional candidates in 1980, and 59 percent voted for Democratic congressional candidates in 1982.

President Reagan was not uniformly popular with Catholics—or other Americans—throughout his first term in office. While he began with high marks, his popularity plummeted during the 1982 recession and in response to "Reaganomics," his combination of steep budget and tax cuts. When Reagan's popularity was down, it was particularly low among Catholics.

At his lowest point, in January 1983, only 37 percent of Catholics and 39 percent of Protestants approved of the President's performance in office, while 54 percent of Catholics and 52 percent of Protestants disapproved; 67 percent of Catholics and 61 percent of Protestants disapproved of his handling of the economy; 76 percent of Catholics and 71 percent of Protestants disapproved of his handling of unemployment; 51 percent of both Catholics and Protestants said Reaganomics would hurt them personally; 56 percent of Catholics and 51 percent of Protestants said it would hurt the country. Trial heats for the 1984 presidential race taken in February 1983 showed a decided Democratic preference among Catholics.

In a February 1983 poll, Catholics supported Walter Mondale over Reagan by 54–35 percent, while Protestants were evenly split, backing Reagan by 45–43 percent. In the same poll, Catholics supported Senator John Glenn, of Ohio, over Reagan by 48–35 percent, while Protestants gave each candidate 44 percent.

In May 1983, 57 percent of Catholics and 51 percent of Protestants said they did not want President Reagan to run for reelection. But two developments turned the President's popularity around. One was the U.S. invasion of Grenada, in the fall of 1983. Reagan said the raid was needed to protect U.S. citizens on the island from a violent Marxist government that had just staged a coup against another Marxist government. The move was highly popular; in November 1983, Catholics approved by 60–33 percent, Protestants by 61–30 percent. The second development was the economic recovery that began in the middle of 1983. As the economy improved, Catholics and Protestants gave the President similar approval ratings. (See Appendix.)

By May 1984, 60 percent of Catholics and 53 percent of Protestants approved of Reagan's performance in office. Reagan's higher approval ratings affected trial heats and eventually the election itself. Catholics continued to maintain Democratic leanings: In the summer of 1984, they preferred the Reagan-Bush ticket over the Mondale-Ferraro ticket by only 3 to 5 points, while Protestants preferred the Republicans by 17 to 21 points. In our final preelection poll, however, there was, for the first time in the history of the Gallup Poll, no difference at all between Catholic and Protestant views: both preferred Reagan-Bush to Mondale-Ferraro by 61–39 percent. A major factor in Reagan's increase in support among Catholics seems to have been his agreement to hold a summit meeting with Soviet Premier Mikhail Gorbachev in an effort to make a breakthrough in arms-control talks. Up until that point, Reagan had remained vulnerable with Catholics on the peace issue; in early 1984, Catholics had said that Mondale was more likely than Reagan to prevent World War III by 50–33 percent, while Protestants saw no difference between the two, with 39 percent picking each man. Nevertheless, in the summer of 1984, 72 percent of Catholics and 67 percent of Protestants said the world was not safer than it had been four years before.

Exit polls conducted on Election Day did find a difference from the final preelection Gallup survey, with Catholics voting for Reagan by 56–44 percent and Protestants by 67–33 percent. There are two explanations for these differences with the Gallup preelection survey. First, they are close to the statistical margin of error for samples of that size. Second, there is a historic tendency for Catholics to vote more Democratic and Protestants to vote more Republican on Election Day than

they show in late polls; there seems to be a "coming home" effect in the
voting booth. But there is no doubt that Ronald Reagan's victory level
among Catholics in 1984 was historic. His popularity level soared after
the election:

	Catholics	Protestants
1/85	58–31	65–27
8/85	64–27	69–23
9/85	69–23	60–31
10/85	66–27	63–29
1/86	64–26	65–27

But, in the same pattern that we saw during his first term in office,
President Reagan's overall approval rating was considerably higher
than his approval rating on specific policies. (Consider the findings from
October 1985 in the Appendix.)

The most common explanation given for this phenomenon is that
Americans simply like and trust Reagan personally and like the way he
stands up for what he believes, even when they themselves disagree.
That is certainly part of the explanation, but we believe there is also
something more: It is quite possible that the gap between Reagan's
overall approval rating and his rating on specific issues indicates a confidence on the part of Americans—and particularly Catholics, who are
still less supportive of Reagan on specific issues than are Protestants—
that they can temper Reagan policies of which they disapprove. If this is
the case, it can be seen as a significant sign of confidence in the American political system.

Catholics give Reagan high ratings when asked how history will
judge him; 50 percent say he will be judged as outstanding or above
average (12 percent say outstanding). But that is still 9 points lower
than the 59 percent of Protestants who give him a similar rating (16
percent say outstanding); 12 percent of Protestants and 14 percent of
Catholics say below average or poor.

There is little doubt that Reagan's popularity, particularly when
viewed alongside Carter's lack of popularity, is responsible for a heavy
shift toward Republican affiliation among Catholics. The political affiliation of American Catholics remained remarkably stable between 1965
and 1977. But, between 1977 and 1984, the number of Catholics citing
Republican allegiance more than doubled, rising by 18 percentage

points, from 14 to 32 percent; Republicans gained 12 points among Protestants during this same period. Republicans gained five points among Catholics during the 1980 campaign and held that gain, and picked up another 12 percent during 1984.

By the third quarter of 1985, the percentage of Catholics citing Republican affiliation had slipped back to 29 percent, but the Democratic share had dropped to a modern low of 38 percent. In the last quarter of the year, however, Democrats made a significant gain, moving to a 44–30 edge, their best showing since early 1984. It is too soon to tell whether this means that Republicans have peaked among Catholics and that more traditional patterns are reemerging.

Political affiliation is only one measure of attitudes toward political parties. Equally important are attitudes about which party is best for peace, best for prosperity, and best for handling the most important problem facing the nation. The Republicans have made major gains in all these areas during Reagan's first term in office. Between 1980 and 1985, the Republicans picked up 12 points among Catholics as the party best able to keep the peace. But, significantly, the Democrats still hold a 41–32 percent lead among Catholics as the party best for peace, while Protestants pick the Republicans by 42–30 percent.

Catholics now regard the Republicans as the party best for prosperity, although by a smaller margin—45–35 percent—than Protestants, who pick the Republicans by 50–35 percent.

Similarly, the Republicans have made substantial gains as the party best able to handle the most important problem facing the nation; here, Catholics (38–28 percent) and Protestants (41–31) both pick the Republicans by a 10-point margin. What is also significant here is that there is no significant difference in the way Catholics and Protestants perceive the most important problem facing the nation; Catholics sometimes rank unemployment and international tensions and fear of war higher than do Protestants, but the pattern is not consistent.

Another way to measure attitudes toward the two parties is to ask Americans which party is better for particular groups of people. Catholics and Protestants both see the Republicans as best for business and professional people, white collar workers, and skilled workers; they both see the Democrats as best for small-business people, farmers, retired people, the unemployed, women, union members, unskilled workers, and blacks. In almost every instance, Catholics are more likely than Protestants to view the Democrats as the party best for whichever group is mentioned.

POLITICAL AFFILIATION

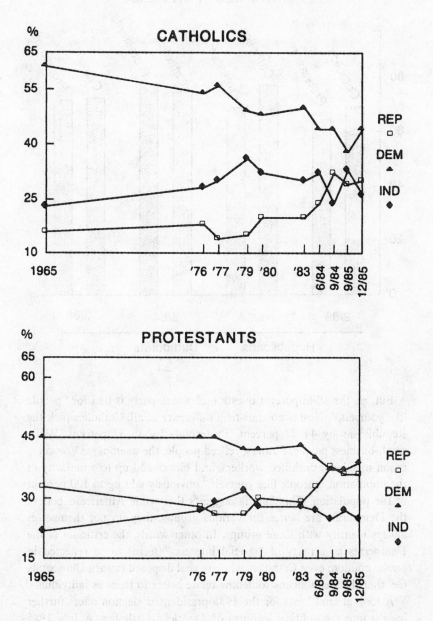

CATHOLICS

REP
□

DEM
▲

IND
◆

PROTESTANTS

REP
□

DEM
▲

IND
◆

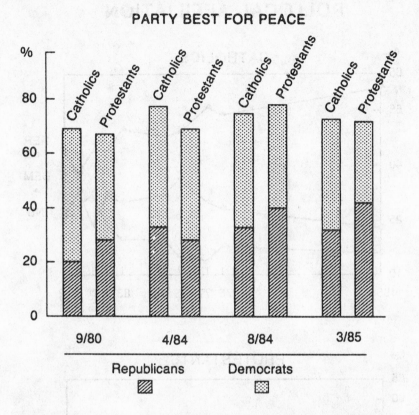

PARTY BEST FOR PEACE

Republicans   Democrats

But, on the all-important question of which party is best for "people like yourself," there is no statistical difference at all: Catholics pick the Republicans by 44–37 percent, Protestants by 45–37 percent. While small-business people, farmers, retired people, the unemployed, women, union members, unskilled workers, and blacks add up to a majority of the population, "people like yourself" obviously add up to 100 percent of the population. This finding suggests that while Americans believe the Democrats are better for various groups, they do not themselves always identify with those groups. In other words, the criticism of the Democrats as a party of "special interests" seems to be reflected in public opinion; even Catholics who are well disposed toward Democrats feel that the Republicans somehow relate better to them as individuals.

A look at trial heats for the 1988 presidential election offers further insight into the political leanings of American Catholics. A July 1985

PARTY BEST FOR PROSPERITY

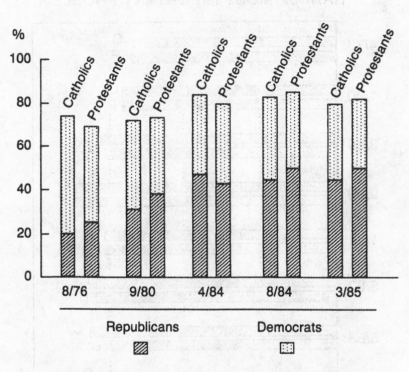

series of trial heats among registered voters found Vice President George Bush leading all Democratic contenders except Senator Edward Kennedy, of Massachusetts, among Catholics; they also showed Catholics leaning more Democratic in other matchups, including those of Bush with Senator Gary Hart, of Colorado, and New York governor Mario Cuomo, a Catholic:

	Bush	Kennedy
CATHOLIC	39	53
PROTESTANT	54	40
TOTAL	46	46
	Bush	Hart
CATHOLIC	46	43
PROTESTANT	54	37
TOTAL	50	39

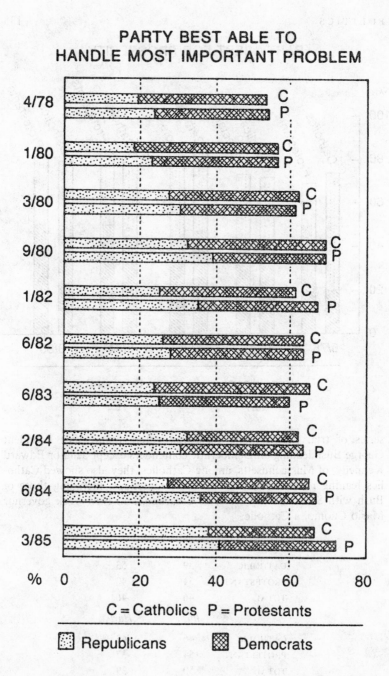

PARTY BEST ABLE TO
HANDLE MOST IMPORTANT PROBLEM

C = Catholics   P = Protestants

Republicans   Democrats

	Bush	Cuomo
CATHOLIC	48	38
PROTESTANT	62	25
TOTAL	55	31

After Senator Kennedy announced that he would not run in 1988, Hart moved into a virtual tie with Bush and a lead among Catholics. Catholics also remained more Democratic than Protestants in other matchups:

	Bush	Hart
CATHOLIC	39	53
PROTESTANT	50	44
TOTAL	45	47

	Bush	Cuomo
CATHOLIC	50	41
PROTESTANT	59	29
TOTAL	54	31

CONCLUSION

There is no doubt that a sea change has occurred among the political loyalties of American Catholics—and within a very short time. Republicans have a degree of support and respect among Catholics that is unheard of in modern times. But they do not yet command a plurality of support among Catholics—and they may not reach that stage. Democratic loyalties remain deep among Catholics—though not as deep as Republican loyalties seem to remain among white Protestants—and Catholics still have very positive feelings about the party.

Perhaps the most interesting phenomenon about shifting political loyalties among Catholics is that they have not become more conservative as they have become more Republican. In fact, they have become more liberal on foreign-policy issues and still see the Democrats as the party best for peace; they have maintained their liberalism on economic issues, and their support for government social programs still puts them closer to the Democratic platform than the Republican; while they are conservative, in political terms, on some social issues, such as abortion, school prayer, and tuition tax credits, where the Republicans have the advantage, they are liberal on other social issues, like women's rights and civil rights, where they are closer to the Democrats.

In his 1977 book *Religion at the Polls,* Albert J. Menendez wrote that about 20 percent of Catholics were Republican and that they were "conservatives à la William F. Buckley." That assessment may well have been correct in 1977—but it would not be correct today. To the degree that Catholics have become Republican, they are moderate and liberal Republicans; the new Catholic Republicanism is the Republicanism of the suburbs, not of conservative ideologues.

Catholics drawn to the Republican Party in the 1980s have been drawn by an economic recovery, the force of Ronald Reagan's personality and can-do attitude, improved relations with the Russians, and stepped-up arms-control talks; they have been repelled by a sense that Democrats are appealing to everyone else but them. Ironically, they have been drawn to the Republicans as President Reagan has done things normally associated with Democrats: reducing unemployment and conducting arms-control talks.

The climate is right, however, for a Democratic renaissance among Catholics: Democratic registration seems on the rise, solid majorities of Catholics continue to vote Democratic in local elections, and Catholics remain highly compatible with Democrats on most issues. The days of Democratic presidential candidates garnering more than 70 percent of the Catholic vote are gone, but a strong candidate could hope to hit 60 percent, and one who came close could also expect to attract enough Protestants to be elected.

XII. HISPANIC CATHOLICS

Throughout the last part of the twentieth century, the Catholic Church in the United States will face few challenges as great as that of ministering to the growing Hispanic population in its midst. Hispanics present a sizable minority from a different culture with a large number of low-income people and a large percentage of new immigrants. As if those factors did not present a sufficient challenge to the Church, it must also deal with an external challenge: massive efforts by Evangelicals, Pentecostals, and Jehovah's Witnesses to convert Hispanic Catholics to their religious beliefs. A 1978 Gallup study of Hispanic Catholics conducted for *Our Sunday Visitor,* a Catholic weekly, found that an incredible three quarters—74 percent—had been approached by Evangelicals, Pentecostals, or Jehovah's Witnesses in an attempt to convert them. The figures might well be even higher today, given the fact that awareness of the challenge by the Church is much higher than it was a decade ago. Churches trying to attract Hispanic Catholics, for the most part, believe Hispanics' spiritual needs are not being met by the Catholic Church.

All Hispanics in the *OSV* survey were asked their opinion of these religious groups, regardless of whether or not they had been approached by them. While a plurality, 45 percent, said they had no opinion of these groups, one third of Hispanics—35 percent—had a favorable impression. Only 20 percent had negative feelings. Furthermore, opinions of these groups were remarkably uniform, with no particular demographic groups in the Hispanic population having substantially differing views on this subject.

Fundamentalists and others have targeted Hispanic Catholics because they are generally more interested in religion and in an emotional style of religion than other Catholics and often are not fully integrated into the Catholic community. We do not have sufficient data to gauge how successful these groups have been in converting Hispanic Catholics; a study done several years ago for the Archdiocese of New York found that 10 percent of Hispanics had converted to another religion after coming to the United States. Hispanics make up 7 percent of the U.S. population; 70 percent are Catholic, 18 percent are Protestant, 3 percent cite other religious affiliations, and 9 percent have no religious ties. Hispanics make up 16 percent of American Catholics, some 10.5 million people.

Father Anthony Bellagamba, former executive director of the U.S. Catholic Mission Council, says U.S. churches financially support and are coordinated with overseas efforts, particularly in Central and Latin America. Church sources agree on the major problem groups: There are no problems with mainline Protestant groups, with whom the Catholic Church carries on an ecumenical relationship; there are problems with some, though not all, Baptist churches. Catholic leaders are particularly critical of the Mormons, sects like the Jehovah's Witnesses, and hundreds of small pentecostal churches. "There's no ecumenism at this level, no respect for substance," says Father Silvano Tomasi, director of the U.S. Catholic Conference Office for the Pastoral Care of Migrants. "They just want bodies." Bellagamba talks of the "venom" with which these groups talk about the Catholic Church in Central and Latin America.

Catholic sources also agree on the tactics the other churches use: First attract poor immigrants with social services, then teach them a Bible-centered theology that rejects the Catholic Church. Catholic leaders speak with a mixture of anger and envy when they talk about the services these churches provide: vans to bring people to and from church and for food and medical care, and plenty of bilingual workers to help the Hispanics get what they need. Sister Margarita Velez, who heads the Hispanic-affairs office for the Archdiocese of Washington, says, "For the Hispanic, Christ is Christ and the Bible is the Bible. They go to these churches for the social services, and then they [the sects] proselytize. At the beginning, they don't attack the Catholic Church. But, little by little, they give them the Bible and say, 'We don't believe anything outside the Bible.' " Paul Sedillo, USCC secretary for hispanic affairs, says, "They find a Hispanic community leader, indoctrinate him and underwrite a church for him—he brings along a whole community."

Tomasi says the Evangelicals will redefine the "unchurched" in a nominally Catholic country producing immigrants: "They'll say 5 percent Catholic, 1 percent Protestant, 90 percent unchurched. Once you start with defining these as unchurched, they become the object of a duty on behalf of believers. Sometimes Catholics go along with these definitions—they'll say, 'They're not really Catholics.' Well, they're not 'perfect Catholics.' But the Irish and Italian and German immigrants who came to this country had the same kind of religious education— they all came from a poor, rural background. That does not mean that the values of Catholics are absent—community, faith, redemption, the Church. We can't judge them by the standards of the upper middle class."

Tomasi says the small fundamentalist churches attract Hispanics looking for a sense of community: "People want a sense of community. Traditionally, the church has been doing it. If we don't, they will find a way. The first step is the need for a group, then comes the rationalization for the move."

According to Tomasi, the Church's concern about defecting Hispanics is not about numbers, but about theology. "They create a kind of ideology of 'Me and God.' The community dimension of response to others disappears. It becomes a political statement, a move to right-wing politics—there's no concern for the poor, no sense of collective responsibility."

The Catholic Church has been doing more than complaining, however; some in the Church are trying to meet the challenge posed by the fundamentalists. Referring to their emphasis on social services, Tomasi says, "There's absolutely nothing wrong with it. We are not sensitive enough to do it as our official documents say we must. The New Code of Canon Law says every baptized person has the right to be ministered the sacraments and preached the word of God in his own language." Tomasi notes that earlier generations of immigrants began with national parishes: "There were 2,000 German-language parishes, 1,700 Polish parishes, more than 1,000 Italian parishes."

Tomasi says it isn't necessary to duplicate that experience, but it is necessary to allow the immigrants to form a community within a community in order to achieve full integration in a generation or two. He concedes that it is easier for fundamentalist churches and sects to develop indigenous Hispanic leaders, because they don't have to worry about celibacy or eight years of seminary training. But, he says, "In the Catholic community, we can still develop leadership and responsibility. We have married deacons and give them a greater role. We're developing full-time catechists who spend their whole time evangelizing. It works. Celibacy is not the main issue. There are now options for leadership."

Our data do suggest that Hispanics are generally happy with the Catholic Church. But they are also vulnerable to conversion efforts because of their curiously loose institutional attachments. While Hispanic Catholics appear to be a devout people in many respects, they see the Church primarily as a place of worship, rather than a source of direct help or comfort with personal, family, or community problems. Hispanics also seem to be vulnerable to conversion efforts that stress the Bible and indigenous Hispanic leadership.

The "Gallup Study of Religious and Social Attitudes of Hispanic-Americans," conducted for *Our Sunday Visitor,* is the most comprehensive Gallup survey ever conducted of Hispanic Catholics. Although some changes have no doubt occurred in religious attitudes and practice in the intervening period, the study remains a valuable source of information, providing, for example, a breakdown of the ethnic backgrounds of Hispanic Catholics:

MEXICO	54
SPAIN	13
PUERTO RICO	12
CUBA	11
SOUTH AMERICA	6
CENTRAL AMERICA	3
DOMINICAN REPUBLIC	3

It is quite likely that the proportion of Hispanics from Central America is higher today than in 1978 because of the influx of refugees from the war-torn region in the 1980s. Here are some other demographic facts about Hispanic Catholics, most from the *OSV* study:

▪ Hispanics prefer to be identified by their specific background, as Cubans or Mexican-Americans; only 8 percent preferred the label "Latino," and 4 percent each preferred "Hispanic" or "Chicano."

▪ Hispanic Catholics believe, by 53–36 percent, that they are treated as well as other groups in the United States. The most satisfied group is made up of Cubans in the Southeast: 75 percent say they are treated as well as other groups; the least satisfied group is made up of Puerto Ricans in the East: 50 percent say they are not treated as well as others.

In general, younger Hispanics are less satisfied than their elders with their treatment in society. Two thirds of Hispanics believe that various groups of Hispanics get along well with one another. Here, again, Cubans in the Southeast have the most positive attitude, while Puerto Ricans in the East have the least positive attitude.

▪ 29 percent of Hispanic Catholics live in the Pacific region, 30 percent in the Southwest and Rocky Mountain states, 10 percent in the Midwest, 10 percent in the Southeast, and 21 percent in the East.

▪ Hispanics lag considerably behind a national sampling of Catholics in income. In 1978, only one Hispanic Catholic in five had an income above $15,000 a year. This was half the figure for Catholics as a whole.

▪ A plurality of Hispanic Catholics are Democrats in about the same proportion as all Catholics; they are less Democratic in orientation than are black Catholics.

▪ 56 percent of Hispanic Catholics say they usually speak Spanish in the home, 23 percent speak English, and 20 percent speak both.

There is considerable reason to believe that Hispanic Catholics are a devout people. In the *OSV* survey, 64 percent of Hispanic Catholics said religion was "very important" to them; this was 10 points higher than the response among a sample of Catholics in general the same year. One very important finding emerging from the survey was that religion appears to be of primary importance to women, the elderly, and those in down-scale economic groups. It would appear that as Hispanic-Americans become more assimilated into American society and more affluent, religion will become a less important factor in their lives.

Only 57 percent of those in the *OSV* survey said they would describe themselves as "good Catholics," while 37 percent said they would not describe themselves that way. The approximately six in ten Hispanics who consider themselves good Catholics correlates with the percentage of Hispanics who say they attended church two or more times in the past thirty days: 29 percent had not attended at all in that period, 8 percent had attended once, 11 percent twice, 7 percent three times, 36 percent four times and 7 percent five or more times.

The *OSV* survey found that talking about religion was the only religious practice engaged in by half of Hispanic Catholics in the thirty days before the survey.

A comparison of several questions which overlapped with a Gallup study of a national sampling of Catholics conducted for the Catholic Press Association finds that Hispanics are more likely than other Cath-

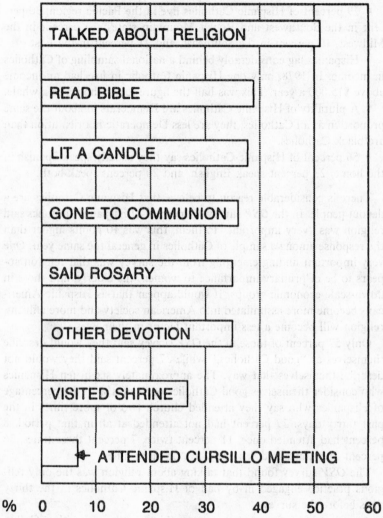

ACTIVITIES OF CATHOLICS
IN LAST 30 DAYS

TALKED ABOUT RELIGION

READ BIBLE

LIT A CANDLE

GONE TO COMMUNION

SAID ROSARY

OTHER DEVOTION

VISITED SHRINE

ATTENDED CURSILLO MEETING

% 0   10   20   30   40   50   60

olics to read the Bible and about equally as likely to say the rosary. Findings from a 1986 update of the CPA study found little difference between Hispanic and white Catholics in religious practice; Hispanics (20 percent) were only half as likely as non-Hispanic Catholics (40 percent) to say they had meditated during the past month. While the 1986 sample of Hispanics was too small to be definitive, it did suggest that Hispanic Catholics—as well as black Catholics—are more involved than whites in the Charismatic Renewal movement. In the *OSV* survey, 23 percent of Hispanics said they were interested in the Charismatic Renewal. Although this was on the low end of the interest scale, it still represents a sizable showing and suggests that the Catholic Church can firm up Hispanic membership by making Charismatic groups available to them. Interest in other areas indicates that Hispanics place a high priority on religious music, art, and literature, as well as Bible study.

The majority of Hispanics (52 percent) believe that, as a group, they have enough say in church affairs in the United States. A significantly large proportion, however, are not satisfied. One third of the Hispanic population (30 percent) do not believe they have enough say in the affairs of the Catholic Church, and an additional 18 percent have no opinion. Responses by demographic groups are fairly uniform, but young people were the most satisfied; college-educated Hispanics and those earning more than $20,000 a year were less satisfied than the average.

The vast majority of Hispanics (78 percent) would like to see more Hispanic culture and tradition included in church services. Although all demographic groups are clearly in favor of this, some statistically significant differences are found within some groups. For example, women are more in favor (82 percent) of increasing Hispanic culture and tradition in church services than men (74 percent). Those with the lowest income and least education are more likely to want more Hispanic influence on church services; those with the highest incomes and most education are least likely.

Asked what they like best about the church they attend most often, Hispanics are most likely to cite parts of the church service itself:

Like best about church

THE MASS/COMMUNION	19
THE PEOPLE/ATMOSPHERE/UNITY	16
THE PRIEST/THE WAY HE HELPS US/GOOD ADVICE	11

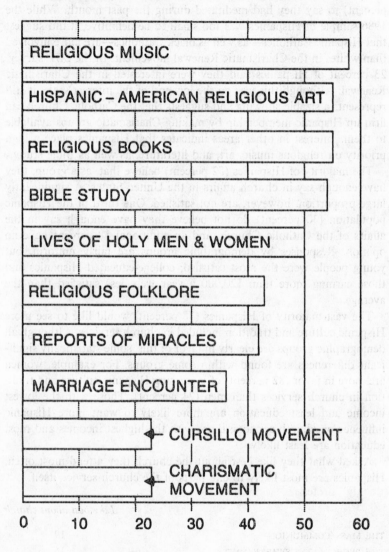

INTEREST OF CATHOLICS IN
RELIGIOUS SUBJECTS AND ACTIVITIES

RELIGIOUS MUSIC

HISPANIC – AMERICAN RELIGIOUS ART

RELIGIOUS BOOKS

BIBLE STUDY

LIVES OF HOLY MEN & WOMEN

RELIGIOUS FOLKLORE

REPORTS OF MIRACLES

MARRIAGE ENCOUNTER

CURSILLO MOVEMENT

CHARISMATIC MOVEMENT

0   10   20   30   40   50   60

Like best about church

LIKE EVERYTHING ABOUT IT	10
SERMONS	6
CHORUS/RELIGIOUS MUSIC	5
USE OF SPANISH LANGUAGE	3
PHYSICAL ASPECTS OF THE CHURCH	3
TEACHINGS/THE FAITH ITSELF	3
SOCIALIZING/MEETINGS/PROGRAMS/BIBLE STUDY	3
OPENNESS/FREEDOM TO EXPRESS FEELINGS	2

Hispanics had far fewer negative feelings about their own church: when asked what they liked least about the church they most often attended, only one in three could name anything. Another third could not name anything they didn't like and the final third said specifically that there was nothing that they didn't like. Two thirds of the criticisms raised fell into the miscellaneous category, which means that there were not enough instances of any one complaint to warrant its own category. Specific complaints raised were as follows: too much emphasis on collections, too many changes in recent years, and no feeling of belonging with the people there—3 percent each—and poor treatment by the priest and too much noise—2 percent each.

Hispanics clearly want more Hispanic priests and deacons: 69 percent want more Hispanic deacons and 76 percent would like more Hispanic priests in the United States; among those who feel Hispanics do not have enough say in the Church, 83 percent want more Hispanic priests. Two thirds of Hispanics—65 percent—believe the lack of educational opportunities is an important reason for the small number of Hispanic priests in the United States. The next-most-cited reason was the ban on marriage for priests: 49 percent said this was an important reason for the low number of Hispanic priests. Hispanics were evenly divided on another issue, with 45 percent saying the fact that a man had to leave his family for training was a factor and 45 percent saying that it was not. Only one third (36 percent) said the priesthood was not a "manly" profession; half (56 percent) denied this. Only 29 percent of Hispanics believe that discrimination against Hispanics is a factor; 59 percent do not believe that this is an important reason.

While 76 percent of Hispanics want to see more Hispanic priests, only 56 percent say they would want a son of theirs to become a priest. This drops to 46 percent among those aged eighteen to twenty-four. A slightly smaller percentage of Hispanics (51 percent) want a daughter of theirs to become a nun.

The *OSV* survey found that Hispanics believe, by 49–34 percent, that their parish priest is interested in their personal lives, but only 7 percent say they turn to the Church for help when they have a problem. Given this reluctance to turn to the Church for help, it is not surprising that fully half of Hispanics say the Church has never given them help with a problem. It seems that Hispanics do not see the Church's role as a helper in such situations. Of those who have been helped by the Church with a problem, the largest group (23 percent) say the Church helped by providing moral and spiritual guidance.

Half of the Hispanics surveyed (54 percent) could not name a community problem they thought their church should do more to deal with. Of those Hispanics who can suggest community problems their church should do more about, most name problems concerning youth: 14 percent mention counseling youth and 9 percent suggest their church should provide youth programs. Seven percent suggest family and marriage counseling. Among the more traditional church functions, helping the poor (11 percent), the elderly (7 percent), and the sick (6 percent) are also mentioned.

There are other indications of weak Hispanic ties to the institutional church. Only 10 percent of those surveyed said they were currently doing some kind of work for their church, although another 41 percent said they would be willing to do some work if they were asked. The 1986 survey on religious practice among Catholics found that Hispanics were less likely than other Catholics to have attended a Catholic social function or a meeting of a Catholic organization in the past thirty days; this suggests that Hispanics feel somehow distant from those functions and organizations.

CONCLUSION

As we have seen, Hispanic Catholics generally feel very positive about the Catholic Church; but those good feelings are somewhat tenuous: Church leaders must firm them up by training more Hispanic leaders, allowing Hispanics greater say in the Church, integrating more Hispanic culture and traditions into church life, providing better Bible study, and integrating Hispanics more fully into church life.

XIII. TEENAGE CATHOLICS

Up until now, we have been examining the attitudes of adult Catholics. But, over the past decade, the Gallup Teen Survey has collected a considerable amount of information about the attitudes and beliefs of American teenagers. This information allows us to take a closer look at the world in which teenage Catholics live—a world often very different from that inhabited by their parents. It also allows us to look at a new generation growing up in a society in which surface differences between Catholics and Protestants are disappearing. One of those narrowing differences involves the religious makeup of the age group; as we noted earlier, while Protestants outnumber Catholics two to one among adults, the ratio is much narrower, about four to three, among teenagers.

Another way in which we can see the similarity of Catholic and Protestant teens is by looking at the common backgrounds of the parents of today's teenagers: four in ten of both Catholics and Protestants come from families in which the chief wage earner is either a professional or a business executive; four in ten of both have fathers who have completed college or beyond; 33 percent of Protestants and 28 percent of Catholics have mothers who have completed college or beyond. More than eight in ten among both Catholic and Protestant teens plan to attend college.

One important clue that we can obtain from surveys of teenagers is the degree to which patterns that differentiate adult Catholics and Protestants are being passed along to their children. We simply do not have enough data to compare adults and teens on every issue. But it is possible to draw some conclusions; some Catholic-Protestant differences are clearly being passed along to the next generation, but there are clear signs that other differences may not be. One pattern that does seem to be passed on is the Protestant emphasis on going it alone. In a survey on values, 80 percent of Protestant teens said that independence was "very important" to them; at the same time, only 66 percent of Catholic teens cited independence as "very important."

A second pattern being passed along to teenagers is a greater Catholic permissiveness concerning sex, alcohol, and marijuana. For example, in a survey asking teens what social changes they would welcome, 69 percent of Catholics and 55 percent of Protestants said they would welcome greater acceptance of sexual freedom. This is consistent with a number of findings about attitudes of Catholic adults, particularly the finding that Catholics are considerably more likely than Protestants to believe that there is nothing immoral about premarital sex: 58 percent of Catholic and 46 percent of Protestant adults approve of premarital sex.

Catholic teens differ from Protestant teens in two other ways where sex is concerned. First, Catholic teens (32 percent) are more likely than Protestants (23 percent) to give an "A" to the quality of sex education they receive in school:

RATE QUALITY OF SEX EDUCATION

	Catholics	Protestants
A	32	23
B	33	42
C	23	20
D	7	5
F	4	5

Catholic teens are also more likely than Protestant teens to say they get their most accurate information about sex from their teachers—and less likely to say they get it from their parents. Interestingly enough, while the figures are small, Catholic teens are more likely to say they get the most accurate information about sex from religious leaders—surprising, given the fact that Catholic teens want more sexual freedom, while their religious leaders preach traditional values and are celibate.

SOURCE OF MOST ACCURATE INFORMATION ABOUT SEX

	Catholics	Protestants
PARENTS	34	45
FRIENDS	23	26
TEACHERS	25	18
RELIGIOUS LEADERS	7	2
BOOKS/ARTICLES	14	15

Catholics are also passing on a greater acceptance of the use of alcohol to their children. Catholic teens are more likely than Protestants to drink: 52 percent of Catholic teens and 40 percent of Protestant teens say they have had a drink within the past week; 18 percent of Catholics and 15 percent of Protestants say liquor has at some time been a cause of trouble in their families. There is no significant difference, however, in the percentage of Catholic and Protestant teens who say they have driven after drinking: one in five in both groups admit to doing so. In addition, 31 percent of Catholic and 25 percent of Protestant teens have been passengers with drivers who had been drinking.

Adult attitudes toward liquor are being passed on in another way: Protestant teens are more likely than Catholic teens to view alcohol as dangerous. For example, Catholic teens view marijuana as more dangerous than alcohol by 53–31 percent, while the ratio among Protestants is only 50–40 percent. And while a slight plurality of Catholic teens—48–44 percent—believes that cigarettes are more dangerous than alcohol, Protestants by 52–40 percent believe that alcohol is more dangerous.

Paralleling attitudes among adults, Catholic teens are slightly more tolerant of marijuana use than are Protestant teens; 14 percent of Catholic and 9 percent of Protestant teens say they would welcome greater acceptance of marijuana use. Marijuana use, which in many ways was symbolic of the youth values of the '60s, has lost considerable support among teens. In 1979, one teen in four (24 percent) argued for greater acceptance of marijuana use, but in 1985, the proportion had dropped to only one in nine (11 percent).

The declining approval of marijuana may be related to the fact that there is a consensus among Catholic and Protestant teens that the biggest problem facing people their age is drug abuse, with 38 percent of Catholics and 43 percent of Protestants citing it as the main problem. The next-greatest problem is alcohol abuse: 14 percent of Catholics and

17 percent of Protestants cite this problem. While teenage suicide does not appear on this list, it is obviously a real concern to teenagers: 46 percent of all teenagers say they know someone their age who has tried to commit suicide. Catholic teens (51 percent) were slightly more likely than Protestant teens (44 percent) to say they know someone their age who has attempted suicide; this difference may well be due to the fact that Catholics are more likely to live in urban areas, where they simply know more people than do those living in rural areas.

Catholic and Protestant teens also agree that drug abuse is the major problem facing the public schools. Here, they both differ from their parents; adult Catholics and Protestants view lack of discipline as the major problem in the schools, while teens believe the biggest problem is drug use. Among teens, however, Catholics are twice as likely as Protestants to view lack of discipline as the biggest problem.

BIGGEST PROBLEM FACING PUBLIC SCHOOLS

	Catholic		Protestant	
	Teens	Adults	Teens	Adults
USE OF DRUGS	29	18	34	20
LACK OF DISCIPLINE	13	28	6	29
PUPILS' LACK OF INTEREST/ TRUANCY	10	6	10	4
INTEGRATION/ SEGREGATION	2	2	5	3
LACK OF PROPER FINANCIAL SUPPORT	8	9	11	9
DRINKING	4	3	5	3
CRIME	7	2	4	1

A final Catholic-Protestant difference being passed down to today's teens is a lower Catholic priority on religion. There are some similarities between Catholic and Protestant teens: four in ten in both groups are receiving some form of religious instruction. (This percentage is interesting in light of the fact that more than three Americans in four say they want religious education for their children.) And the lesser Catholic emphasis on religion must be seen in the context of the fact that Catholic teens are more likely than Catholic adults to attend church and read the Bible.

If parents are not doing a particularly good job of seeing that their children receive religious instruction, they are at least getting them to attend church. Among Catholics, 51 percent of adults and 64 percent of teens say they have attended church in the past seven days; 39 percent of Protestant adults and 59 percent of Protestant teens say they have attended church in the past seven days. Among teenagers, Protestants are almost as likely as Catholics to have attended church in the past week, but there is a larger gap among adults. It remains to be seen whether this means that this generation of teenagers will be more likely to continue attending church as they grow older, or whether the drop-off in church attendance is simply greater among Protestant young adults than among Catholics.

Parents also seem to be able to get their children to read the Bible. This is not surprising among Protestants: Protestant teens and adults are about equally likely to read the Bible often. But while Catholic teens are still less likely than Protestant teens to read the Bible, they are more likely than Catholic adults to read it: Catholic adults are almost three times as likely to say they never read the Bible; 35 percent of Catholic teens and only 25 percent of Catholic adults read the Bible at least once a week. Again, it will take time to see whether this is simply a reflection of parent-induced religious education in teens or the sign of a real shift in practice. But it is relevant to point out that we have already noted a sharp increase in Bible reading among adult Catholics under thirty.

Despite high levels of church attendance and Bible reading, both Catholic and Protestant teens show a high level of belief in superstitions; a somewhat larger percentage of Catholic teens (82 percent) than Protestants (75 percent) are likely to believe in at least one item on a list of superstitions.

SUPERSTITION BELIEVED IN

	Catholics	Protestants	Total
GHOSTS	21	19	20
LOCH NESS MONSTER	16	20	18
BIGFOOT	21	29	24
WITCHCRAFT	23	24	22
ESP	57	64	59
CLAIRVOYANCE	25	32	28
ANGELS	69	74	69
ASTROLOGY	58	56	55

FREQUENCY OF BIBLE READING

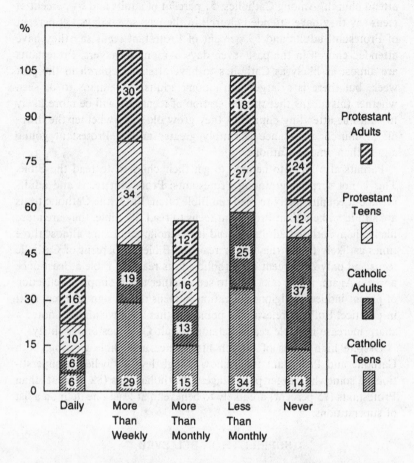

A related finding is that 11 percent of Catholic teens and only 2 percent of Protestant teens say they read books about the occult, supernatural, or horror. This could be related to the slightly greater Catholic tendency to believe in superstition, or it could reflect the fact that many horror stories, like *The Exorcist,* have Catholic themes.

Again, despite high levels of church attendance and Bible reading among Catholic teens, only 11 percent say that religion is the most important influence on their lives; the figure is 26 percent for Protestants.

HOW INFLUENTIAL ARE RELIGIOUS BELIEFS ON YOUR LIFE?

	Catholics	Protestants
MOST IMPORTANT	11	26
ONE OF MOST IMPORTANT	59	50
ONE OF LEAST IMPORTANT	20	15
LEAST IMPORTANT	9	8

A final important finding in the area of religious belief and practice is that a plurality of Catholic teens say that religion is less important to them than it is to their parents: 42 percent say it is less important, 30 percent say it is more important, and 26 percent say they place about the same degree of importance as their parents on religion. Protestant teens are more evenly divided: 36 percent say religion is more important to them than to their parents, 37 percent say it is less important, and 23 percent say it is about the same.

There is an obvious contradiction between the fact that Catholic teens are more likely than their parents to go to church or read the Bible, yet still say religion is less important to them than it is to their parents. It could signal that Catholic teenagers are really not getting very much out of their religious experience. Teenagers are to some extent a captive audience where religion is concerned, and the figures for church attendance and Bible reading may simply reflect that.

There is one Catholic-Protestant difference in which there has been at least a temporary breakdown between the generations: in the area of political affiliation. Among adults, a plurality of Catholics cite Democratic affiliation and a plurality of Protestants cite Republican affiliation. Among teens, however, Catholics also show a decided Republican preference. Catholic teens showed a Democratic preference in previous polls, but this switched sharply in early 1984, and Republican gains have held. There is statistically no difference between Catholic and Protestant teens in political affiliation. This is a historic shift.

It is far too early to tell whether this really indicates a long-term effect. In the short run, it is clear that the political perceptions of American teenagers have been shaped by the contrast between the Democratic Carter administration, which they perceived as ineffective, and the Republican Reagan administration, which they perceive as more successful. It may take until after the Reagan era to see how long the shift toward Republicanism lasts.

While Catholic and Protestant teens hold similar views, there is a

POLITICAL AFFILIATION OF TEENS
(REPUBLICANS)

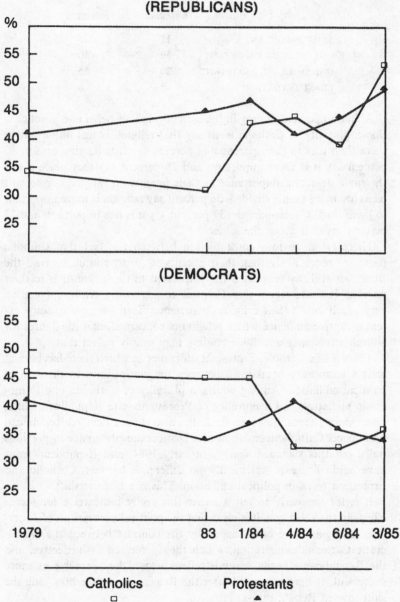

(DEMOCRATS)

Catholics · Protestants

striking difference between Catholic and Protestant teens in their views of the future. When asked whether things will be better or worse ten years from now in the city where they live, Protestant teens are more optimistic than Catholic teens; this may reflect the urban concentration of Catholics and a sense that the future of big cities is not bright. But when the focus shifts to the nation and the world, Catholic teens become considerably more optimistic; while both groups are optimistic about the future of the United States, Catholics are more so. And when it comes to the condition of the world ten years from now, Catholic teens believe by 34–26 percent that it will be better than it is today, while Protestant teens believe by 36–28 percent that it will be worse.

10 YEARS FROM NOW

	Catholics		Protestants	
	Better	Worse	Better	Worse
CITY	28	28	33	18
U.S.A.	47	18	35	28
WORLD	34	26	28	36

There are also very tentative signs of another shift among Catholic teenagers: a possible erosion of concern about family life. For example, in one survey, 62 percent of Catholic and 70 percent of Protestant teens said that being able to spend time with their families was very important to them in choosing a career. This was the top choice for both groups. But while it would be wrong to make too much out of the 8-point gap between Catholic and Protestant teens on this issue, it deserves our attention. We would have expected to see the same percentage of Catholic as Protestant teens, and perhaps 2 or 3 points more, say that being able to spend time with their family was "very important." This finding could be evidence of a trend some observers have anticipated: a new emphasis on work, income, and achievement, perhaps at the expense of family life, among young Catholics.

In a more general way, we find that today's teenagers are apparently striving to create a new set of values that combines the traditional Protestant ethic, the social movements of the 1960s, and the characteristics of an affluent postindustrial society. Traditional values, such as greater respect for authority and more emphasis on closer family ties, have never been stronger among the country's teens. At the same time, however, teens also desire more emphasis, in the future, on greater self-expression and the acceptance of sexual freedom. Technological progress traditionally has been respected in America, and although many young people rejected this concept in the 1960s, technology now has won widespread acceptance among teens. The majority of teens believe that there should be less emphasis on money, but there is a slight movement toward the concept that there should also be less emphasis, in the future, on hard work.

In their quest to combine both traditional and modern values, most teens (92 percent) would especially welcome more respect for authority in the future. Within the structure of law and order, eight teens in nine (89 percent) also would like to see more emphasis on self-expression. Eighty-six percent of teens want closer family ties, with only slightly greater emphasis placed on this value among young women (90 percent) than among young men (82 percent). At the same time, a majority of teens (59 percent) also want to see more acceptance of sexual freedom. Young men (65 percent) are more likely than young women (54 percent) to say they want more sexual freedom in the future.

One reason for the desire for stronger traditional family ties seems to be the prevalence of divorce in today's society. The natural parents of one in four of today's teens—including one in four of Catholics as well as of Protestants—have been separated or divorced. Catholic teens (80 percent) are slightly more likely than Protestant teens (71 percent) to say that it is too easy to get a divorce today, but three in four in both groups say that most divorced people did not try hard enough to save their marriages.

Although the values expressed by teens may, on first examination, appear to be contradictory, opinion about them has grown stronger in recent years. The desire for more respect for authority rose from 87 percent in 1979 to 92 percent in 1985. During the same period, the proportion of teens wanting stronger family ties rose from 80 percent in 1979 to 86 percent in 1985; there was an even greater rise in opinion favoring more sexual freedom, from 48 percent in 1979 to 59 percent in 1985.

In 1979, 78 percent of teens wanted more emphasis on technology; now, 86 percent want to see technology play a greater role in the future. The majority of teens (61 percent) would like to see less emphasis on money, but only 39 percent say they would like to see less emphasis placed on working hard. These values may be eroding, however, since, in 1979, only 28 percent said there should be less emphasis on working hard. During the same period, the desire for less emphasis on money dropped only a statistically insignificant 2 percent. Younger teens (thirteen to fifteen) are the most likely to say they want to see less emphasis on hard work in the future (44 percent), and the least likely to believe that there should be less emphasis on money (58 percent).

PERCENT WHO WOULD WELCOME SOCIAL CHANGES

	Catholics	Protestants	Total
MORE RESPECT FOR AUTHORITY	94	93	92
MORE EMPHASIS ON SELF-EXPRESSION	89	89	89
MORE EMPHASIS ON TRADITIONAL FAMILY TIES	88	89	86
MORE EMPHASIS ON TECHNOLOGICAL IMPROVEMENTS	88	85	86
LESS EMPHASIS ON MONEY	60	60	61
MORE ACCEPTANCE OF SEXUAL FREEDOM	69	55	60
LESS EMPHASIS ON WORKING HARD	41	37	39
MORE ACCEPTANCE OF MARIJUANA USE	15	9	11

Teens' responses to another question about values also reveal a clear Catholic-Protestant consensus, with just a few fascinating differences. Although both Catholic and Protestant teens rank religious faith at the bottom of the list, Catholics are less likely to say religious faith is "very important." Interestingly enough, Catholic teens seem a bit more well disposed toward the "Protestant work ethic," with 86 percent rating hard work as "very important," compared to 79 percent for Protestants.

VALUES—VERY IMPORTANT

	Catholics	Protestants	Total
RESPONSIBILITY	93	97	95
HONESTY	93	96	94
SELF-RESPECT	87	88	87
HARD WORK	86	79	82
SELF-RELIANCE	76	81	78

	Catholics	Protestants	Total
INDEPENDENCE	66	80	74
PATIENCE	74	75	74
RELIGIOUS FAITH	49	57	51

There is also considerable consensus of Catholic and Protestant teen-agers on the values that are important to them in choosing a career. Both Catholic and Protestant teens are statistically as likely to rank helping the disadvantaged and earning lots of money as "very important."

VERY IMPORTANT IN CHOOSING A CAREER

	Catholics	Protestants	Total
SPENDING TIME WITH FAMILY	62	70	66
EARNING LOTS OF MONEY	50	54	54
MEETING MANY NEW PEOPLE	50	49	52
HELPING DISADVANTAGED	47	51	49
WORKING WITH HANDS	34	39	38
CONTINUING STUDY AND EDUCATION	33	38	35
HIGH TECH	30	39	34
TRAVELING A LOT	27	30	29
WORKING OUTDOORS	16	23	22
WORKING ALONE A LOT	12	13	13

CONCLUSION

The picture of American Catholic teenagers that emerges is one of confusion and conflict—a natural state for teenagers. Catholic teens are growing up in far more affluent surroundings than did their parents; they are considerably more Republican politically, but not necessarily more conservative. They have picked up some values from their parents, particularly permissiveness in the areas of sex, alcohol, and drugs. Catholic teens, like their parents, place less emphasis than Protestants on independence and rank family values high. But those family values may well be at odds with sexually permissive attitudes and an emphasis on career advancement.

There is similar conflict in Catholic teens' attitudes toward religion.

Their level of church attendance and Bible reading is higher than that of Catholic adults, yet religion is less important to them than it is to their parents.

Research into the religious life of American teenagers is still in its infancy; more questions need to be asked over a longer period of time, and we need to track changes in attitudes of teenagers as they go through the life cycle. But even within this framework, it is clear that Catholic teenagers are growing up in a world that is neither the world of their parents nor the world of other teenagers.

XIV. ALIENATED CATHOLICS

Decades ago, they were called "lapsed Catholics"—those who no longer practiced their faith, or, which was regarded as almost the same thing, stopped attending church regularly. The word "lapsed" placed the burden on those who had "fallen away." Today, the same people are described as "alienated Catholics," with the word "alienated" shifting the burden to the Church, with the suggestion that it has somehow turned its people away. In the post-Vatican II era, the Catholic Church in the United States has turned its attention to "evangelization," understood primarily as wooing back "alienated Catholics."

It is understandable, of course, that church leaders would want as many Catholics as possible to participate fully in the congregational and sacramental life of the Church. But it may well be that they have been looking at a glass and calling it half empty when it could just as easily be called half full. In fact, the picture of "alienated Catholics" that emerges from our studies shows that this is a group that has far from written off Catholicism. "Alienated" or "inactive" or "unchurched" Catholics in many ways do not look much different from active, churchgoing Catholics.

There are several ways to define inactive or unchurched Catholics. One simple way is to compare the 52 million Catholics counted in the Official Catholic Directory with the 28 percent of the American people who identify themselves as Catholic, a figure that works out to approximately 67 million people. This leaves a gap of 15 million unchurched. In a pioneering study, "The Unchurched American," conducted by the Gallup Organization for a coalition of denominations and religious groups in 1978, the unchurched were defined as those who were not members of a church and who had not attended church in the past six months except for weddings, funerals or special holidays like Christmas, Easter, or Yom Kippur. Using that definition, 41 percent of American adults—61 million people—were unchurched. Eighteen percent of those—about 11 million people—were Catholic. In a 1985 study conducted for the National Catholic Evangelization Association, we defined the unchurched as those who have attended church or synagogue less than two times in the past year. Using that definition, 24 percent of American Catholics—about 16.5 million people—are unchurched.

Before we look closer at the more recent survey, we should first review key findings about the unchurched from the earlier survey. Demographically, the unchurched are younger and more likely to be male and single than the churched.

Some of the major differences in attitude between the churched and the unchurched come in areas of personal freedom, generally on sexual issues, and on abortion. For example:

- 21 percent of the churched and 35 percent of the unchurched believe: "The rules about morality preached by the churches and synagogues today are too restrictive."

- 39 percent of the churched and 61 percent of the unchurched believe "it should be possible for a pregnant woman to obtain a legal abortion if she is married and does not want any more children."

- 74 percent of the churched and 53 percent of the unchurched believe extramarital sex is always wrong.

- 19 percent of the churched and 37 percent of the unchurched would welcome "more acceptance of sexual freedom."

The churched seemed to find life more satisfying:

- 48 percent of the churched and 31 percent of the unchurched strongly agreed that: "Facing my daily tasks is a source of pleasure and satisfaction."

- 45 percent of the churched and 31 percent of the unchurched agreed strongly that: "I have discovered clear-cut goals and a satisfying life purpose."

Not surprisingly, there was a dramatic difference between the churched and the unchurched in their level of confidence in organized religion: 80 percent of the churched and only 38 percent of the unchurched reported a great deal or quite a lot of confidence in organized religion. Twenty-four percent of the unchurched said they had very little or no confidence in organized religion. But, interestingly enough, while the unchurched were only half as likely as the churched to give a high confidence rating to organized religion, the Church still ranked

CHURCHED*

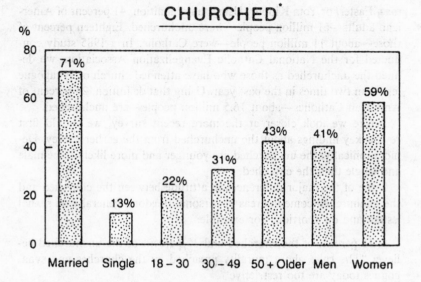

Married	Single	18 – 30	30 – 49	50 + Older	Men	Women
71%	13%	22%	31%	43%	41%	59%

UNCHURCHED*

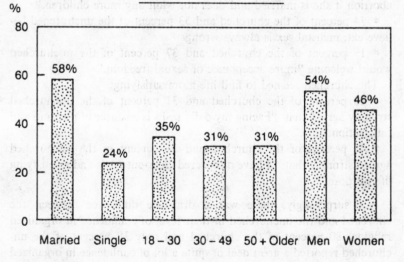

Married	Single	18 – 30	30 – 49	50 + Older	Men	Women
58%	24%	35%	31%	31%	54%	46%

*Total Sample

fairly high among other institutions. Only banks (51 percent) and the
military (45 percent) received a clearly higher confidence rating, and
the unchurched bunched organized religion in the next tier along with
the public schools (39 percent) and the Supreme Court (39 percent).

The "Unchurched American" study found that the unchurched were
critical of the churches; but it also found that large numbers of the
churched held the same criticisms:

	Churched		Unchurched	
	Agree	Disagree	Agree	Disagree
MOST CHURCHES AND SYNAGOGUES TODAY HAVE LOST THE SPIRITUAL PART OF RELIGION	52	38	60	18
MOST CHURCHES AND SYNAGOGUES TODAY ARE NOT EFFECTIVE IN HELPING PEOPLE FIND MEANING IN LIFE	39	46	49	27
MOST CHURCHES AND SYNAGOGUES TODAY ARE NOT CONCERNED ENOUGH WITH SOCIAL JUSTICE	32	43	39	25
MOST CHURCHES AND SYNAGOGUES TODAY ARE NOT WARM AND ACCEPTING OF OUTSIDERS	28	57	37	35

The unchurched cited these as their major problems with the Church:

TEACHINGS ABOUT BELIEFS WERE TOO NARROW	37%
TOO MUCH CONCERN FOR MONEY	32
MORAL TEACHINGS WERE TOO NARROW	28
A DISLIKE FOR THE TRADITIONAL FORM OF WORSHIP	26
I WANTED DEEPER SPIRITUAL MEANING THAN I FOUND IN A CHURCH OR SYNAGOGUE	19
DISSATISFACTION WITH THE PASTOR OR RABBI	18
A FEELING THAT THE CHURCH OR SYNAGOGUE WASN'T WILLING TO WORK SERIOUSLY TO CHANGE SOCIETY	16

Again, not surprisingly, 70 percent of the churched and only 30 percent of the unchurched said that religion was "very important" in their
lives. But there was considerably more agreement on two other signifi-

cant questions: 70 percent of the churched and 88 percent of the unchurched said: "A person can be a good Christian or Jew if he or she doesn't attend church or synagogue"; 76 percent of the churched and 86 percent of the unchurched said: "An individual should arrive at his or her own religious beliefs independent of any churches or synagogues."

The unchurched display a significant degree of religious belief:

- 76 percent say they pray to God.
- 38 percent say they have made "a commitment to Christ."
- 70 percent believe the Bible was either the "actual" or the "inspired" word of God.
- 64 percent believe that Jesus Christ was God.
- 57 percent believe in life after death.
- 24 percent say they have had a "religious experience."
- 74 percent say they want their children to receive religious instruction.
- 43 percent of those with children under eighteen say they have a child receiving religious instruction.

One conclusion to be drawn from the "Unchurched American" study is that churchgoing is a habit learned at home. For example, the unchurched were more likely to have parents who did not attend church frequently.

MOTHER ATTENDED CHURCH

	Frequently	Occasionally	Never
CHURCHED	73	20	4
UNCHURCHED	49	31	14

FATHER ATTENDED CHURCH

	Frequently	Occasionally	Never
CHURCHED	55	27	14
UNCHURCHED	31	28	32

Seventy-seven percent of the unchurched received religious instruction as children, compared to 88 percent of the churched. The churched were more likely to have received religious instruction at home and to have attended religious or parochial school.

The influence of family extends to spouses; the unchurched were considerably more likely to have a husband or wife who did not attend church regularly: 39 percent of the unchurched said their spouse never attended church.

SPOUSE ATTENDS CHURCH

	Every week	More than monthly	Special holidays	Never
CHURCHED	47	37	7	7
UNCHURCHED	10	29	19	39

And, finally, the unchurched are likely to have close friends who do not attend church regularly:

FRIENDS WHO ATTEND CHURCH OR SYNAGOGUE ON A REGULAR BASIS

	All/Most	Some	None
CHURCHED	58	33	5
UNCHURCHED	15	45	24

One of the most fascinating findings of the study was that 23 percent of the churched had had a period of two years or more in which they did not attend church except for special holidays. This strongly suggests that a like percentage of those now unchurched could well come back to the Church at a later date; in fact, 34 percent of the unchurched themselves had not yet been away from church for two years. The return of many of the unchurched seems particularly possible when we see most of the reasons people cite for not going to church. Commenting on the study, Dean Hoge of Catholic University said: "The proportion of Americans who are unchurched for philosophical reasons is not great. Other forces seem to be more determinative, such as interpersonal influences, community relationships and lifestyles."

Here are the reasons those who have been away from church (except for special holidays) for more than two years cite for not attending:

	Churched	Unchurched
WHEN I GREW UP AND STARTED MAKING DECISIONS ON MY OWN, I STOPPED GOING TO CHURCH	22%	34%

	Churched	Unchurched
I MOVED TO A DIFFERENT COMMUNITY AND NEVER GOT INVOLVED IN A NEW CHURCH	32	20
I FOUND OTHER INTERESTS AND ACTIVITIES WHICH LED ME TO SPEND LESS AND LESS TIME ON CHURCH-RELATED ACTIVITIES	34	26
I HAD SPECIFIC PROBLEMS WITH, OR OBJECTIONS TO, THE CHURCH, ITS TEACHINGS, OR ITS MEMBERS	22	19
THE CHURCH NO LONGER WAS A HELP TO ME IN FINDING THE MEANING AND PURPOSE OF MY LIFE	12	19
I FELT MY LIFESTYLE WAS NO LONGER COMPATIBLE WITH PARTICIPATION IN A CHURCH	9	14
POOR HEALTH	9	5
WORK SCHEDULE	14	14
DIVORCED OR SEPARATED	3	5

One of those taking part in the "Unchurched American" study was Paulist Father Alvin Illig, an expert in Catholic evangelization. Referring to the 23 percent of the churched who had been away from the Church for two years or more, he said, "This says to me that with tactful effort, with sensitivity, with patient listening and understanding, with genuine love and with the power of the Holy Spirit, many, many millions of the 61 million unchurched Americans will 'come back home' . . . Most of the reasons for leaving as well as most of the reasons for returning deal with human factors, factors which are often manageable if we are but sensitive to the bruises, the needs, the yearnings, the inadequacies of the churchless."

In 1985, the Gallup Organization conducted a survey of "Attitudes of Unchurched Americans Toward the Roman Catholic Church" for Father Illig's National Catholic Evangelization Association. As noted earlier, this survey defined the unchurched as those who had not attended church twice in the past year. According to this study, 33 percent of all Americans, 30 percent of Protestants, and 24 percent of Catholics are unchurched. Thirteen percent of the unchurched—4.3 percent of the total population—said they once belonged to the Catholic Church, but left. This does not include former Catholics who have converted to another denomination and are "churched" by our survey definition. Five percent of unchurched Protestants say they once belonged to the Catholic Church but left.

But the breakdown of the "unchurched" Catholics raises some interesting questions. For example, 12 percent of this group say they have never belonged to the Catholic Church. This suggests a group of almost two million people who have never had formal church membership, but still, probably because of parental affiliation, identify themselves as Catholics—a group that would seem to be likely, perhaps even willing, subjects for evangelization and an invitation to formally join the Church.

A second category of unchurched Catholics—and the largest—is the 64 percent who say they still belong to the Church, even though, by self-description, they attend Mass less than twice a year. This is very encouraging news for the Church: it means that two in three "unchurched" Catholics do not feel themselves cut off from the Catholic community. This group, too, seems likely to respond positively to an invitation to greater church involvement. The size of this group is also a reminder that people move in and out of the "inactive" category without changing their sense of identity; the line between active and inactive Catholics is not sharp.

The third category of unchurched Catholic, and in many ways the most interesting, is the 24 percent—almost four million people—who say they once belonged to the Catholic Church but left. But four in ten (39 percent) of all those unchurched who say they left the Catholic Church say they have thought of rejoining the Church. This, again, is a finding church leaders should regard as encouraging.

The unchurched Americans who say they once belonged to the Catholic Church but left cite five major reasons for leaving:

1. *Lack of interest in the Catholic Church or religion in general.*

"I just got away from it" is the way a Florida woman described her drifting away from Mass attendance. "I have no interest in attending church" was the comment of a twenty-six-year-old professional man.

2. *They could not accept certain church teachings.*

A thirty-year-old man from Connecticut said, "There were philosophical differences that I had with the Church on such matters as abortion, birth control, general moral issues." A forty-six-year-old salesman from California said, "I don't believe in some of the principles of the Church, such as being condemned to hell for minor infractions of the rules." A fifty-seven-year-old New York housewife said, "The Church has changed its rulings, and I don't agree with this." A twenty-nine-year-old California woman in a managerial position cited "the Church's attitude on birth control." A twenty-four-year-old professional man cited "disagreement with the role of women in the Church, abortion, celibacy, and premarital sex."

3. *They were divorced.*

People citing this reason sometimes place different emphasis on describing it. A thirty-four-year-old Michigan housewife says, "I was divorced"; a forty-six-year-old craftsman from Florida says, "Divorce separated me from the Church."

4. *They felt the Church was getting too far away from the Bible.*

"My religion is the Bible," said a sixty-five-year-old California woman. A twenty-eight-year-old semiskilled workman from New York said, "The study of the Bible taught me different doctrines that they don't teach." A thirty-year-old Texas woman complained, "Most of the time, the priest didn't talk about the Bible."

5. *They objected to what they saw as the Church's emphasis on money.*

A thirty-four-year-old woman clerical worker from Michigan complained, "They were concerned about money more than human problems." A twenty-nine-year-old professional man from Pennsylvania said he was "tired of overemphasis on money and donations to the Church." "I'm dissatisfied with the stand the Church took on the political issues," said a forty-two-year-old manager from New York.

Even though the specific instances differed, some of the comments reflected a sense of having been hurt and turned away by the Church. A sixty-year-old woman service worker from West Virginia said, "Because I married outside the Church, I was disowned by the Church"; a retired seventy-seven-year-old woman from Washington said, "The priest said I wasn't married, because I wasn't married in the Catholic Church." A fifty-nine-year-old Massachusetts woman said, "After a relative of mine had joined the Jehovah's Witnesses, his daughters upon his death were asked by the priest to confess that their father had sinned."

The six in ten unchurched Catholic dropouts who say they would not consider returning to the Church cite these reasons:

1. 62 percent said they cannot accept some of the Church's teachings.

2. 15 percent cited negative factors relating to priests: 7 percent said they did not feel comfortable going to a priest, 5 percent said they felt the priest would not be responsive, and 3 percent said they had gone to a priest and been turned away.

3. 14 percent said the Catholic way of life is too demanding.

4. 7 percent said the whole process of joining the Catholic Church is too complicated.

5. 7 percent said, "I am divorced and remarried and therefore cannot join the Catholic Church."

Here are the top ten reasons cited by all of the unchurched for joining the Catholic Church:

1. *God exists and is the creator of everything* (22 percent). The implication here, of course, is that regardless of the different paths to God, the all-important, underlying, unifying principle is a God whom all Christians worship.

2. *Sense of family: emotional and moral support among Catholics* (20 percent). This figure is statistically identical to the first figure and represents one of our most significant findings. The Catholic Church clearly offers something Americans today are seeking: supportive and dependable fellowship. We have found in recent international surveys that Americans are the loneliest people in the world and are in search of a feeling of community.

3. *Catholic relatives, friends, or neighbors* (18 percent). This underscores the point that evangelization programs should begin close to home.

4. *Marriage between a man and a woman is lifelong* (14 percent). Despite the high divorce rate in the nation, Americans want their marriages to succeed. Even the divorced believe that marriage partners ought to try harder to save their marriages. The Catholic Church's belief in the indissolubility of marriage offers a strong support for marriage to many Americans.

5. *Jesus Christ is both true God and true man* (8 percent).

6. *Jesus Christ is alive today and is lord and savior of all people* (8 percent). These findings highlight the centrality of Christ in reaching the unchurched and seem to suggest that evangelization efforts should give a greater emphasis to the "living Christ," which is an ingrained belief of both Catholics and Protestants.

7. *Human life is sacred* (7 percent).

8. *Religious instruction for children and youth* (7 percent). This finding reflects the fact that many Americans who have drifted away from the Church themselves think about returning, because they want religious instruction for their children. Today this is known in church circles as the return of the "Baby Boom" generation, but it describes a phenomenon that seems likely to affect young adults of all generations.

9. *There is a Heaven and a Hell, and all people will eventually go to one or the other* (6 percent). Underlying this response may be a feeling of concern on the part of some that Americans are losing their sense of sin.

10. *People and nations are required to work sincerely for peace* (6 percent). This finding suggests that the U.S. bishops' pastoral letter *The Challenge of Peace* may have stirred further thinking on the urgent need for peace in the world.

There were some interesting differences among Catholic and Protestant unchurched in the reasons they cited for joining or not joining the Catholic Church. First, Catholic responses were higher across the board: for example, 36 percent of unchurched Catholics cited their belief that "God exists and is the creator of everything" as a reason to consider rejoining the Church. Unchurched Catholics were more likely than unchurched Protestants to cite reasons for return which reflect a broader social, communitarian concern: 14 percent said, "Each person must be concerned for the poor and act to help them"; 12 percent said, "The Ten Commandments and the Beatitudes of Jesus are important guides for morality"; 12 percent said, "People and nations are required to work sincerely for peace." None of those three reasons was cited by as many as 6 percent of unchurched Protestants, who were more attracted by the centrality of Christ and belief in the existence of Heaven and Hell; 7 percent cited the fact that "in moderation, people can smoke, drink, play cards, dance, etc."

Here are the top ten reasons the unchurched cited for not joining the Catholic Church. The negative factors seem to cluster around sex-related issues such as artificial birth control, abortion, and sex outside of marriage. These will be the key issues with which Catholic evangelizers will have to deal through the turn of the century and beyond.

1. [The Church's teaching that] *the use of mechanical and chemical means to limit birth is wrong* (21 percent).

2. [The Church's teaching that] *abortion is wrong* (20 percent).

3. *The Catholic Church and* [its] *use of money* (16 percent). This has been a persistent criticism of the Church, but it is still surprising that it receives the third-highest number of mentions as a factor keeping people from joining or rejoining the Church. It's interesting to note that Catholics are considerably less likely (8 percent) than Protestants (22 percent) to give one tenth of their income or more to the Church. Perhaps this information can be useful in dealing with that stumbling block.

4. *The Pope as universal shepherd of all Catholics* (12 percent). This reason for not joining or rejoining the Church may be based upon misinformation; for example, the mistaken belief that every statement uttered by the Pope is to be taken as absolute law.

5. *Statues, rosary, incense, holy water, candles, medals, etc.* (10 percent).

6. [The Church's teaching that] *sex outside marriage is wrong* (9 percent). While younger and older Catholics are in agreement in their opposition to extramarital sex, younger Catholics are considerably more supportive of premarital sex.

7. [The Church's teaching that] *marriage between a man and a woman is lifelong* (9 percent). This is the only factor to be cited as a reason for both joining and not joining the Catholic Church; if its citation as a reason to join reflects support for the institution of marriage, its citation as a reason to not join probably reflects concern with a perceived lack of sympathy for those who do choose divorce.

8. [The Church's teaching that] *the Church has the right to teach on controversial religious matters* (7 percent). The authority of the Church is a stumbling block to some, but it is perhaps worth observing once again that many Americans, while not agreeing with the Church's position on certain issues, nevertheless appear to believe that it must set ideals or goals toward which one is to strive.

9. *Church buildings* (7 percent). This is probably not a comment on Catholic architecture, but a reflection of concern about the church and money and discomfort with statues, candles, and so on.

10. *Devotion to Mary and the saints* (6 percent).

Unchurched Catholics were more likely to cite abortion, birth control, and issues related to church authority; surprisingly, 6 percent—the tenth-most-mentioned reason—cited "Catholic relatives, friends, or neighbors" as a reason not to rejoin the Church. Unchurched Protestants were more likely to cite more cultural reasons: papal authority, devotion to Mary and the saints, statues, etc.; 8 percent cited the Vatican itself and the international structure of the Catholic Church, and 7 percent cited Catholic church buildings.

An analysis of "The Unchurched American," "Attitudes of Unchurched Americans Toward the Roman Catholic Church," and other studies suggests a number of courses of action the Church could take which would lead both unchurched Catholics and other unchurched Americans to join, rejoin, or become more fully involved in the Catholic Church:

1. *Reevaluate religious education programs.* To the extent one is able to judge an institution by its product, one could ask certain questions about the quality of religious education in America today. Sunday school and religious education classes have been called by some "the most wasted hour of the week." Whether or not this is true is a question for debate, but the fact remains that nearly as high a percentage of the unchurched as the churched have attended Sunday school. Survey evidence indicates that many adult Americans—including those who have attended religious education classes—are shockingly ignorant about the Bible and key facts about their religion. Church leaders might well ask these questions about their religious education programs: Are children learning the basic facts about their religion? Is the program enriching their religious and spiritual lives? Is the curriculum suited for each particular age level? Are teachers dealing with character formation in young people? Are children acting out their beliefs in real-life situations?

2. *Reexamine the status of religion in the home.* One of the greatest differences between the churched and the unchurched is that the churched are more likely to have had religious education in the home and are more likely to have had parents who attended church frequently. While many religious leaders argue that the home should be the center of religious education, the facts clearly indicate that many parents are not living up to their responsibilities. An effort by clergy to work closely with parents to help shape religious life in the home would be fruitful. Church leaders must ask questions such as: Does the family talk about God and religion? Is the Bible read regularly? Does the family pray together? What is the nature of devotion in the home? Are efforts made to apply Gospel precepts to character formation in the home? What do parents themselves know about their faith? How many

parents, particularly if they themselves do not go to church, can give a good answer to the child's question: "Why should I go to church?"

3. *Priests must be continually sensitized to the impact they have on people.* A large number of Catholics left the Church because of bad experiences with priests, and many are prevented from coming back by fear of similar experiences. There is no way to ensure that such incidents do not occur, but a better-trained clergy in a post-Vatican II environment can limit their number. At the same time, the Church can benefit from spreading the word that the vast majority of American Catholics are happy with their priests; as we saw earlier, in one survey, 74 percent of Catholics gave their pastor an "A" or a "B" grade, and in another survey, 88 percent approved of their priests' performance.

4. *Evangelism tailored to Catholics.* It is impossible to attract large numbers of alienated Catholics and unchurched Americans without a conscious program of evangelization. But it must be a program carefully tailored to the Catholic culture. We have seen that Catholics are considerably less likely than Protestants to evangelize and are turned off by a "hard sell" evangelization style they associate with Evangelicals and other fundamentalists. The best form of evangelization for Catholics is simply an invitation to join a warm, loving parish community. Family members and peers—young people evangelizing young people, and so on—are probably the most effective evangelizers. There is considerable wisdom in the advice of Monsignor William McCormack that the best approach to evangelization is to "propose, not impose."

5. *Reach out to people in a community.* Many people have never been invited to try a new church, but would do so if they received an invitation. As we noted above, Americans today are searching for a sense of belonging, a sense of being part of the community. The finding that 20 percent of the unchurched see a sense of family as a reason to consider joining the Catholic Church suggests an appeal that may have been previously neglected.

6. *Pay greater attention to spirituality.* Many of the unchurched lead active spiritual lives but have not yet found a church that meets their needs. Others are looking for a deeper sense of meaning in their lives and help in clarifying their lives' goals.

7. *Build on—rather than compete with—religious broadcasting.* An increasing number of Americans, including Catholics, get their religion through the broadcast media. Catholics are more likely to watch local religious services and programs than Evangelical programs; local churches would be well advised to develop church programs to supple-

ment and complement local broadcasts with follow-up discussions and commentary.

8. *Evaluate the effectiveness of the Church's mission.* Dioceses and parishes can conduct their own surveys to determine how good a job they are doing of getting their message through to their congregations. The Princeton Religion Research Center has developed a manual to help local churches conduct such surveys.

9. *Run better—and better-publicized—Bible study programs.* Large numbers of Catholics believe their church does not pay sufficient attention to the Bible; they are sensitized to the importance of the Bible by Evangelical groups and broadcasts. At the same time, the emphasis placed on the Bible since Vatican II by the Catholic Church is one of its best-kept secrets. An educational campaign about the Church's emphasis on the Bible would attract a small, but significant, amount of unchurched Catholics and others.

10. *Develop parish programs that appeal to young people, particularly singles and young men.* A disproportionate share of the unchurched are male, single, and under thirty. This is normally a very difficult group to reach, although many do return to church once they start to raise a family.

11. *Improve treatment and awareness of the separated, divorced, and remarried.* Our surveys repeatedly show that the Church's treatment of divorce is a major cause of concern to both active and inactive members; the Church received its lowest marks for its handling of the separated, divorced, and remarried in our church job-performance survey; a large percentage of Catholics would like to see the Church's teaching on divorce changed; and divorce looms as a major reason why people have left or feel unable to rejoin the Church. On a practical level, the Church today is considerably more responsive to the needs of the separated, divorced, and remarried than it has been in the past; many people feel cut off from the Church because of divorce when there is no reason to feel that way.

12. *Education—and candor.* As we have seen in a number of areas, many Americans—Catholics and non-Catholics alike—feel estranged from the Church because of mistaken beliefs about church teachings and attitudes. We have also seen that Catholics give the Church only middling grades on its handling of changes in the Church since Vatican II. An educational campaign to update the perception of the Church and its attitudes toward issues like divorce and the Bible would pay huge dividends—both in terms of enabling many alienated Catholics to

return to the Church and of better informing active Catholics. The Extraordinary Synod of Bishops which met in the fall of 1985 to commemorate the twentieth anniversary of the close of the Second Vatican Council, called for extensive new educational programs on the council's teachings; our surveys clearly show that such an effort is needed.

A certain amount of candor is also needed—and in an area that is obviously very delicate for church leaders. We have seen that most unchurched Americans hold religious views similar to those of churched Americans. But we have also seen that many churched Americans feel the same criticisms of the Church—and the same differences with some key church teachings—as unchurched Americans. For example, while unchurched Catholics are more likely than churched Catholics to disagree with elements of church teaching on birth control, abortion, and divorce, millions of active Catholics share the same disagreements.

CONCLUSION

The U.S. Church has tolerated widespread internal dissent as a means of keeping the Church intact. On a practical level, the only belief that separates many active and inactive Catholics is the belief by active Catholics that they are "in" and the belief by inactive Catholics that they are "out." It would be unrealistic to expect any church to simply invite people in to believe whatever they want to believe. But a candid acknowledgment of the degree of acceptance of responsible dissent within the Church would lead many of those who believe they are "out" to come back "in." Alienated Catholics would not be the only ones helped; the whole Church would benefit from the participation of "unchurched" Catholics, who have a great deal to offer.

XV. CHANGING THE CHURCH AND THE NATION

The American Catholic people are an extraordinary bunch. By virtue of being American, they have reshaped the Catholic Church; by virtue of being Catholic, they have reshaped American society.

Part of what we have seen in this volume confirms that American Catholics practice what has been called a "pick-and-choose" brand of religion, taking from their church what they want and discarding what they do not. This is a very American approach. But what has not been as well appreciated is that by the sheer numbers in which they have adopted this style of loyal opposition, they have forced the American bishops to accept their new definition of Catholicism. Given the widespread dissent from church teaching on such issues as birth control, divorce, and abortion, the U.S. bishops face two basic choices: They could attempt to discipline dissenters; this would entail effectively taking action against perhaps four out of five Catholics in this country, who dissent on at least one major issue. A hard-line attempt of this kind would create massive disruption and unrest within the Church.

The second alternative for the bishops is to accommodate the New American Catholicism; to tacitly accept widespread dissent as the cost of continued unchallenged acceptance as members of the Catholic family. That is the alternative the bishops have, on a practical level, adopted—have, in fact, been forced to adopt by their people. It is a model that makes the Vatican very uncomfortable; that is why there is occasionally a great deal of tension between the Vatican and the American Church. But it is a model that is irrevocably cast. The strongest concentration of conservatism is found among Catholics over fifty. But this is not a case of people becoming more conservative as they grow older; it reflects the attachment of older Catholics to the Church in which they grew up. It is likely that younger Catholics will grow "more conservative" as they grow older only in the sense that they will become more involved in parish activity as they raise families; but these young Catholics are also attached to the Church they know and envision, and they will not become more conservative on issues like women's rights as they grow older. As the pre-Vatican II generation of American Catholics dies off and is replaced by the post-Vatican II generation, the pressure for liberalization within the Church is quite likely to increase.

This does not mean that there is constant tension between the U.S. bishops and their people. They are in many ways remarkably well attuned to one another. While the information in these pages poses some serious challenges for Catholic Church leadership in the United States, we believe that the picture of American Catholics which emerges is far more upbeat and optimistic than most church leaders would expect. In fact, we believe we can refute five major negative stereotypes of American Catholics held by both church leadership and rank-and-file Catholics:

Stereotype 1: *Religious activity is declining dramatically among Catholics.*

Stability and growth—not decline—are the earmarks of Catholic religious life today. The dramatic drop in weekly church attendance from the 1950s to the late 1970s has leveled off; church attendance has been stable for a decade, and the 53 percent of Catholics who say they attended church within the past week is the highest in a decade. In addition, 71 percent of Catholics attend church at least twice a month and 78 percent attend at least once a month, suggesting not that fewer Catholics are going to church, but that they are simply going less often. (On Easter Sunday, 67 percent of American Catholics attend Mass.) At the same time, there has been a sharp increase in Catholic involvement in religious activity outside of Mass; more Catholics are taking part, and those who do are taking part in more activities. Four Catholics in five are involved in such activity. Increases have come in Bible reading, meditation, confession, prayer meetings, saying the rosary, and participating in church organizations and social functions. In fact, the proportion of Catholics saying the rosary—four in ten—and going to confession in the past month—one in four—is the same as it was in 1971.

Stereotype 2: *Young Catholics are leaving the Church.*

Low church attendance and dissatisfaction with the Church among young Catholics reflect a life-cycle impact and the Church's difficulties in ministering to young singles, but they do not indicate that young Catholics are leaving the Church for good. In fact, they seem to be following another life-cycle pattern and returning to church in their late twenties and early thirties as they begin settling down and raising families. The 37 percent of Catholics under thirty who say they went to church in the past week is just about the same as the proportion of all adult Protestants who attend church in a given week. And while Catholics under thirty are still less likely than older Catholics to take part in religious activity outside of Mass, two in three do participate, reflecting a sharp increase since 1977.

Stereotype 3: *The more education Catholics get the more likely they are to leave the Church.* The truth is that college-educated Catholics are the cutting edge of the Church, more involved in the Church and more satisfied by their involvement: 61 percent of college graduates and 55 percent of those with some college attend Mass in a given week; Catholics with a college background are no less likely to be involved in religious practices (except saying the rosary) than Catholics with less education; 60 percent of those with a college background rate the Church as "excellent" or "good" in meeting their needs.

Stereotype 4: *Catholic women are in a state of revolt.* The role of women in the Church is clearly a problem area for church leadership: one Catholic in three gives the Church poor grades in this area; only 8 percent of Catholics believe that a greater role for lay women would hurt the Church; two Catholics in three want to see women ordained as deacons and half want to see them ordained as priests. Yet 61 percent of Catholic women attend Mass in a given week, their involvement in a variety of religious activities is high, and only 7 percent rate the Church "poor" in meeting their own needs. Catholic women want much more from their church; but they have not given up their belief that it is still *their* church.

Stereotype 5: *Catholics have grown more conservative as they've grown more affluent and are not interested in justice and peace issues.* It is true that there has been a dramatic increase in identification with the Republican Party among Catholics—from 15 percent in 1979 to a peak of 32 percent in 1984 and 30 percent in 1985. But this shift does not reflect increased conservatism on major issues. In fact, if anything, Catholics have grown more liberal during that time. Among Catholics, 84 percent support a bilateral nuclear freeze, 77 percent support increased government spending on social spending, 69 percent support the Equal Rights Amendment, and 68 percent want to cut military spending; on these issues and many others, Catholics are more liberal than the general population and are clearly in the liberal camp. This does not mean that bishops and pastors may not encounter resistance to a social-justice agenda in a given place, but it does indicate that Catholic leaders should be encouraged by the basic orientation of their people on these issues.

There are other reasons for church leaders to be encouraged: The level of belief in basic Christian doctrine about the existence of God and the divinity of Christ is quite high. Second, the Church gets better-than-passing grades in its handling of the needs of Catholics: Half (50 percent) of American Catholics give the Church "excellent" or "good" marks for handling their own needs, 37 percent give it a "fair" grade, and only one Catholic in eleven—9 percent—give the Church a "poor" grade. While church leaders would obviously prefer to receive even higher grades, these findings are generally encouraging.

In some specific areas, American Catholics are even more pleased than they are overall. For example, the ten-to-one approval rating for parish priests is really quite remarkable. There is also considerable evidence that the Second Vatican Council has firmly taken root in the Catholic Church in the United States, even in the absence of what the bishops admit was less than optimum education. The Church received one of its highest ratings for its treatment of the role of lay people in the Church. While Catholic lay persons clearly want even more responsibility within the Church, the high level of support for the Church's handling of the issue so far suggests that they understand that lay participation is an evolving process and that lay people are satisfied with the pace of change; conversely, they would become quite dissatisfied if the pace should slow down.

Given the centrality of family life in the Catholic tradition, the bishops can also take some pride in the approval ratings given to their treatment of families. Our surveys also indicate that the elderly are far happier with their treatment by the Church than anyone would have anticipated; they further indicate that those over fifty and retired persons are among the most active in church activities across the board. Given the combination of longer life expectancies and a healthier elderly population—what is known as the "young elderly"—the Church has a broad pool of talent on which to draw. In fact, Catholics from all backgrounds and age groups are willing to become more involved in church life if they are asked to do so. We have seen that there is a great Catholic reluctance to evangelize in the traditional sense of the word, but there should be no similar reluctance to simply invite people with at least nominal parish ties to become more fully involved. In the business world, there are companies that specialize in recruiting people for top-level jobs; if each parish developed a committee to recruit people for a host of parish activities, the result would be a dramatic increase in involvement.

One of our most significant findings is the unusually high level of participation in Catholic church life by men: There is very little difference, apart from the level of Bible reading, between men and women in terms of religious practice such as prayer, meditation, confession, and church organizational activities; 55 percent of men give the Church either an "excellent" or a "good" mark for meeting their needs. The attraction of the Catholic Church for men bears further investigation. We do not believe that the higher level of satisfaction for men comes at the expense of women or because of a perception that women have a second-class status in the Church; in fact, we found that men are even slightly more likely than women to give the Church poor grades for its treatment of women. In general, men rank well behind women on most scales of traditional piety; it may be that the relatively low priority on piety for piety's sake within the Catholic Church and its more intellectual and pragmatic orientation offers a special appeal to men.

There are, however, also serious remaining problems for church leadership. One is divorce. Two Catholics in three want the Church to change its teachings and allow divorced Catholics to remarry within the Church; one Catholic in three gives the Church poor marks for its handling of separated, divorced, and remarried Catholics and the marriage tribunal system; Catholics divorce in the same proportion as the general population, and one Catholic in ten are separated or divorced and single today. The Catholic Church in the United States has come a long way in its treatment of separated, divorced, and remarried Catholics in the past fifteen years; it has displayed a greater pastoral sensitivity and made it somewhat easier to obtain a church annulment. But there is widespread resentment at the process and growing numbers of people who are separated and divorced. Church leaders would be well advised to prepare for a time when divorced and remarried Catholics walk up to the communion rail in the same proportions as Catholics who practice birth control.

Birth control, of course, is the largest symbol of dissent within American Catholicism. Catholics use artificial means of birth control in the same proportion as the general population, and three Catholics in four believe one can practice birth control and remain a Catholic in good standing. But the level of dissent goes far beyond birth control. Catholics are the most permissive major Christian denomination in the nation when it comes to premarital sex; almost two Catholics in three believe there is nothing immoral about premarital sex; one Catholic in three is unwilling to say that extramarital sex is always wrong; one in two believe that homosexuality should be legal. When Catholics view abortion and other "life" issues, they support the Church's position when they view the issue as a matter of "life" and ignore it when they view the issue as a matter of "sex."

The simple fact is that the Catholic Church has not merely lost its credibility on birth control—it has lost much of its credibility on everything related to sex. American Catholics do not disregard church teaching on every issue, but birth control clearly established the pattern that they accept church teaching only when it makes sense in terms of their own situations and their own consciences. When it comes to sex, church leaders are preaching to an audience that is simply not paying any attention. Preaching more loudly or more often or in more sympathetic tones will not change that. Short of changing its teachings on sex, the Church needs a new strategy: young Catholics will not listen to a Church that tells them not to have sex, but they will listen to a Church that tells them that empty sex with a succession of partners is unfulfilling and demeaning; married couples will not listen to a Church that tells them not to practice birth control, but they will listen to a Church that emphasizes responsible parenthood and the need for loving, faithful relationships.

Two other serious problems for the Church we have uncovered come as something of a surprise. One is the extent—the disturbing extent—to which the Catholic Church has become a middle-class church. Many commentators have wondered whether the Church would be able to meet the needs of an increasingly educated and affluent middle-class membership; but the Church may be in danger in meeting the needs of middle-class families so well that it is losing its ability to serve Catholics who do not fit that mold. Two thirds of non-white Catholics give the Church a "fair" or a "poor" rating for meeting their needs; half of

Catholics with family incomes below $15,000 a year (54 percent) give the Church a "fair" or "poor" rating; Hispanics are not fully integrated into church life; three Catholics in five (62 percent) give the Church a poor rating for its handling of the needs of single people. A Church that emphasizes family life must find a way to show that the one Catholic in three who are unmarried are still part of the Church's family; a Church that began in this country as the Church of poor, immigrant working men and women and that proclaims a "preferential option for the poor" must show it has not left the poor and minorities behind in a Church in which one Catholic in five are Hispanic or nonwhite. There is a real danger of the Church's becoming polarized, containing an increasingly affluent white middle class and a struggling minority class who are strangers to one another.

The second surprise comes in the area of the Church's involvement in political and social issues. Here we find a real contradiction: On one hand, a majority of lay Catholics agree with positions taken by the bishops on issues such as arms control, Central America, abortion, education, and economic policy; on the other hand, there is a strong resistance to the Church's being involved in the political arena. This contradiction suggests that the problem lies more with the style of the bishops' political involvement than the substance of the issues involved. First, the bishops have obviously not articulated a clear, simple rationale for speaking out on public issues; second, they have not persuaded their people that they—the bishops—know what they are doing and are not acting, intentionally or otherwise, in a partisan manner. If a prominent bishop, for example, appears to act in a partisan manner—such as by singling out one candidate for criticism, as some did in attacking Geraldine Ferraro's support for legal abortion in the 1984 presidential campaign—he creates the impression that "the bishops" all think that way. This undermines everything else the bishops do in the public-policy arena. American Catholics of all political persuasions do not want their bishops to appear even remotely to be telling them how to vote. The bishops will be successful in building more support for addressing public issues if they can avoid signs of political partisanship.

Our data suggest that there are several opportunities for greater Catholic activity that have not been previously recognized. One is the potential for a significant Catholic push for educational excellence at all levels and in both public and parochial schools. American Catholics give a high priority to education; if church leaders can tap into that support and address education issues in the public arena in a way that does not suggest political partisanship, they can make a major contribution to the state of education in this country.

Another opportunity lies in improved ties between Catholics and mainline Protestants. Relations between these groups do not pose a problem now, but the overwhelming desire of American Catholics for greater ecumenical activity and the previously unrecognized level of cultural and theological affinity between Catholics and Methodists, Lutherans, Presbyterians, and Episcopalians suggest that these churches have only begun to scratch the surface of possible cooperative efforts. At the same time, the gap which emerges between Catholics and Evangelicals suggests the need for greater contact between these groups in order to reduce possible tension between them, especially as the Catholic presence in the South increases.

In several other areas, church leaders face both challenge and opportunity:

■ Hispanic Catholics (64 percent) are more likely than other Catholics to say that religion is "very important" in their lives; they are more likely to attend Mass weekly, and only one in three can find anything to complain about in their local parish. But four in ten say they are not good Catholics; one in three believe Hispanics do not have enough say in how their church is run; Hispanics are not well integrated into their parishes, and three in four have been proselytized by Evangelicals and others who are campaigning hard to attract Hispanic Catholics.

■ Catholic Teens. Catholic teens have a higher church attendance rate (64 percent in the past week) than Catholic adults and are considerably more likely to read the Bible—37 percent of Catholic adults and only 14 percent of Catholic teens say they never read the Bible. But 58 percent believe in astrology and 42 percent say religion is less important to them than to their parents, while only 30 percent say it is more important. It still remains to be seen whether Catholic teenagers have picked up their parents' communal values as well as their permissive attitudes toward sex, alcohol, and drugs.

■ Alienated Catholics. There are about 16 million American Catholics with very loose ties to their church. Their sharpest differences with the Church are on issues related to personal freedom, sexual morality, and abortion. But two thirds do not consider themselves separated from the Church. And of some four million people who say they once belonged to the Catholic Church but left, 40 percent say they have thought about rejoining it.

▪ There has been a sharp increase in the level of Bible reading among Catholics—the number saying they had read the Bible within the past month rose from 23 percent in 1977 to 32 percent in 1986 among all Catholics and from 17 to 32 percent among Catholics under thirty. Hispanic Catholics want more Bible study, and a large proportion of those who left the Church cited lack of attention to the Bible as a major factor. At the same time, there has been a slight increase among Catholics who view the Bible as the literal, not just inspired, Word of God. The good news here is that Catholics are increasingly interested in, and in some cases hungry for, the Bible; the bad news, from the Church's point of view, is the likelihood that the Catholic Church is not really geared up to meet this need and that some Catholics are getting their interpretation of the Bible from fundamentalist Christians who do not share Catholic theology.

Our findings also identify two other areas that bear close watching because they show signs of potential problems that could become quite serious. The first problem involves the regional differences that emerged in religious practice and church satisfaction levels. The best news here concerns the Church in the Midwest, where such archdioceses as Chicago, Detroit, Milwaukee, and St. Paul-Minneapolis have earned the reputation for progressivism within the Church. Our findings show a vital, happy Church in the Midwest: 59 percent attend Mass in a given week, 79 percent take part in some religious activity outside of church in a given month, and 61 percent of Catholics in this region give the Church an "excellent" or "good" rating for meeting their needs. The picture is rosy. The picture is only slightly less rosy in the West. The South ranks high in terms of church attendance and religious practice but lags in approval rating, perhaps because of a larger proportion of minorities. But the region that emerges as a real problem area is the East: only 49 percent of Catholics in the region attend Mass in a given week, the level of participation in religious activities is lower than in any other region, and 55 percent of Catholics in the East give the Church "fair" or "poor" ratings for meeting their needs. The East, led by the Archdioceses of New York, Boston, and Philadelphia, has a reputation as being the most traditional region within the American Catholic Church, with the most hierarchical structure and the lowest level of Vatican II reform. Our findings clearly suggest that areas that have wholeheartedly endorsed post-Vatican II renewal have a happier, more active Church—even when measured in terms of traditional religious practice—than those which were slower to implement the Second Vatican Council.

A second area of potential trouble is Catholic family life. Family life has always been at the heart of Catholicism; we have even noted the surprising finding that the sense of family within the Church is attractive to and a reason for joining the Church by non-Catholics. But there are hints of problems to come. Not one of these findings is definitive in itself; but, taken together, from a variety of approaches, they suggest the approach of a great deal of confusion, upheaval, and even rebellion involving Catholic family life:

- The traditional Catholic preference for larger families has disappeared, with Catholics no different from Protestants in preferring small families.

- Several results from a 1982 survey on satisfaction levels also indicate potential trouble for Catholic families. Catholics were 6 to 12 points less likely than either mainline or Evangelical Protestants or the population at large to give a "10" or a "9" rating—on a scale of 1 to 10 —to their married life or family life. While the difference is small, Catholics even ranked a few points behind other Americans in ranking a good family life as an important value.

- Catholic teens are slightly less likely than Protestants or the general population to say they want to get married when they grow up.

- While Catholic teens rate being able to spend time with their families as the most important criterion for choosing a career, they are slightly less likely than Protestants or the general population to do so.

- There are signs that Catholic women are confused about the role that families should play in their lives. The percentage of Catholic women who described the ideal lifestyle as married with children, with or without a job, dropped from 81 percent in 1982 to 66 percent in 1985; the same surveys showed a 6-point increase in the percentage of Catholic women who saw childlessness as the ideal and a 9-point jump in the percentage of those who are undecided. Those shifts were larger than those found among either Protestants or the general population. While the margin of error in this particular poll was fairly high, it clearly suggests a trend that bears watching.

All in all, our findings indicate that American Catholic church leaders should be more optimistic than they appear to be about the state of American Catholics; at the same time, they need to understand that some of the problems on the horizon are not necessarily ones they have anticipated.

THE CATHOLICIZATION OF AMERICAN CULTURE

When social scientists attempt to explain changes in the Catholic Church in the United States, they often speak about the "Protestantization" of American Catholics, a term normally associated with an emphasis on individual freedom. But Dean Hoge, professor of sociology at Catholic University, argues that it is misleading to talk about the "Protestantization" of American Catholics. "The reason," Hoge says, "is that it implies too much control of American culture by the Protestants. The reality is that Protestant churches today are also caught in the midst of pressures for change which feel like they are coming from outside and (to simplify a bit) *are* coming from outside. Social changes are just as bewildering to Protestant church leaders as to Catholic church leaders. So the sources of the Catholic changes today are deeper and broader in American culture than just the Protestant churches, and the term 'Protestantization' misses this important fact."

Hoge's point is well taken—and we will take it a little further. We agree that it is misleading to talk about the "Protestantization" of American Catholics; but it is also true that American society bears some unmistakable Protestant imprints. The emphasis on individual freedom, democratic structures and participatory democracy, hard work, personal achievement, and the "Protestant work ethic" are all parts of the American culture which have their roots in the predominantly Protestant culture in which our nation was born.

This raises an intriguing question: Have Catholics also helped shape the society which is in turn shaping them? There are only two possible answers: "Yes" and "No." To answer "No" is to say that the largest single denomination in the country, accounting for almost one third of the population and almost one half of the nation's Christians, has been completely passive, absorbing from its culture but contributing nothing to it. Nothing more than common sense dictates that we answer the question "Yes."

But that poses another question: If Catholics have helped shape American society, how have they done it, and in what ways? To answer this question, we turn first to another piece of conventional wisdom about Catholics: that they are "more liberal than Protestants but more conservative than Jews." That statement is accurate, but it, too, is misleading, because it implies a certain "middle-of-the-road" status to Catholics, as though they were the Muzak of denominations. That generality, accurate though it is, obscures the liberalism of American Catholics. If Catholics have made a unique contribution to American society, it must come in the areas in which they differ somehow from American Protestants. We believe that there are areas of important differences and that, in those areas, Catholics have tilted the balance in a direction other than the one in which it would have gone had there not been such a strong Catholic presence in society. On most of these issues, Catholics have been the cutting edge, staking out a position where they were later joined by Protestants.

1. Tolerance. Catholics have helped other Americans become more tolerant of religious, racial, ethnic, and other diversity in two ways. First, by their very presence—as a "minority" denomination in a "Protestant" nation which was larger than any other single denomination, American Catholics literally forced American Protestants to accord them equal rights. Second, Catholics led by example. One of the most dramatic and consistent findings in these pages was the greater tolerance of Catholics than Protestants for diversity—diversity in religion, race, and lifestyle. Even in areas where the gap is small today, such as willingness to vote for a black or a Jew for President, Catholics were more tolerant first. For example, in 1958, Catholics were evenly split (46–45 percent) on whether they said they would vote for a qualified black for President, while Protestants opposed by 58–33 percent. If Catholic attitudes toward blacks had not been more supportive than those of Protestants in the 1960s, the nation would have been far slower to make the civil rights advances it has made since then. The greater Catholic tolerance for atheists, homosexuals, and couples living together outside of marriage is a strong buffer against persecution of such groups. Catholics are aware of their own minority status, sensitive to racial and ethnic differences because of their own ethnic heritage, and tolerant of other religious beliefs because of the accepting, pragmatic, this-worldly focus of their theological beliefs. America is a far more tolerant society than it might otherwise be, because of the contributions of American Catholics.

2. Women's Rights. Catholics have been significantly more supportive than Protestants of the Equal Rights Amendment for more than a decade; Catholics are somewhat more likely than Protestants to say they would vote for a woman running for President, governor, mayor, or member of Congress; they are considerably more likely to think well of a woman's ability to serve as President; a majority of Catholics believe women still face discrimination in employment, while a plurality of Protestants do not. Catholics want women to have equal rights in their church, and they are no less adamant about women having equal rights in society. Catholics have given women's economic rights in American society a significant boost.

3. A Communal Dimension to Society. From support for the New Deal and the Great Society to resistance to the Reagan Revolution, American Catholics have consistently supported an active role for government in meeting the needs of the people; Catholics, for example, were considerably more likely than Protestants to support Lyndon Johnson's Great Society programs. More than three Catholics in four today want greater government spending for social programs, and less than one in five believe we are spending too much for such programs now. This is greater support than is found among Protestants. A related development concerns the labor movement. Catholics have traditionally been more supportive than Protestants of the labor movement and formed the backbone of its support; the movement's fortunes have declined as Catholics have come to regard it as less of an ally and more of a "special interest."

America has been receptive to cooperative action and government social responsibility largely because of the impact of Catholics immersed in a communal vision of society.

4. Presidential Politics. Catholics make up the most important swing vote in American society. When traditional Catholic allegiance to the Democratic Party asserts itself, the Democrats win—or come very close. When the Republicans make substantial inroads into the Catholic vote, they win. Heavy Catholic support made the election of Harry Truman, John Kennedy, and Jimmy Carter possible—and almost elected Hubert Humphrey in 1968. Catholics retained their basic Democratic orientation, but by a smaller margin, in the face of a growth of Republican support in the Ronald Reagan era; they are now a two-party church. They are poised to keep the Democratic Party from going too far to the Left and to keep the Republican Party from going too far to the Right. One thing is clear: no Democrat will ever be elected

President without heavy Catholic support, and no candidate—Democratic or Republican—can take the Catholic vote for granted.

5. Peace. One of the most fundamental changes we have documented is the emergence of American Catholicism as the "peace church" in the United States. American Catholics are not pacifists; but they underwent a conversion experience during the Vietnam War, beginning as more hawkish than the general population and ending up as more dovish—and staying that way. Catholic support for a verifiable bilateral nuclear freeze was a major factor in pushing the Reagan administration back to the negotiating table, and its overwhelming opposition to a military solution in Central America—particularly in the face of heavy initial Protestant support for such a policy—may well have prevented the use of U.S. troops in Central America in the early 1980s. Catholics have been very much on the cutting edge on Central America and in slowing the rapid increase in Reagan-era military spending.

These five areas in which we have seen the "Catholicization of American culture" have moved the United States toward a greater sensitivity to equality, justice, and peace, building upon the values of individual freedom and participatory democracy that were a legacy left by Evangelical and mainline Protestants who shaped the early days of the United States. That is no small achievement, and it is time that the American Catholic people are given their proper recognition for smoothing over some of the rough edges in the "Protestant nation" they came to as immigrants.

APPENDIX

CHAPTER II

GOD LOVES YOU

	Great deal	Some	Hardly
EVANGELICAL	92	8	1
BAPTIST	83	12	1
PROTESTANT	79	16	1
PRESBYTERIAN	76	14	9
LUTHERAN	73	20	*
EPISCOPALIAN	72	22	2
METHODIST	68	25	*
CATHOLIC	65	27	3

DO YOU FEEL YOU HAVE A PERSONAL RELATIONSHIP WITH GOD?

	Yes	No
EVANGELICAL	97	1
SOUTHERN BAPTIST	92	3
BAPTIST	91	6
METHODIST	86	10
PROTESTANT	86	8
CATHOLIC	82	9

DEEPENING RELATIONSHIP WITH GOD

	Very important	Fairly important	Not very important	Not at all important
EVANGELICAL	94	6	*	*
SOUTHERN BAPTIST	76	11	9	4
BAPTIST	73	22	3	2
PROTESTANT	67	22	7	3
METHODIST	56	33	7	3
CATHOLIC	46	37	10	4

CLOSE TO GOD

	Yes	No
EVANGELICAL	95	2
LUTHERAN	89	7
BAPTIST	88	5
PROTESTANT	87	8
PRESBYTERIAN	84	14
CATHOLIC	83	12
METHODIST	82	10
EPISCOPALIAN	81	9

CHAPTER III

CHURCH ATTENDANCE

	Catholic	Protestant
1958	74	44
1961	71	43
1964	71	38
1966	68	38
1967	66	39
1968	65	38
1969	63	37
1970	60	38
1971	57	37
1972	56	37
1973	55	37

	Catholic	Protestant
1974	55	37
1975	54	38
1976	55	40
1978	52	40
1979	52	40
1980	53	39
1981	53	40
1982	51	41
1983	52	39
1984	51	39
1985	53	39

TO NOURISH FAITH: FINDINGS

	Catholic	Protestant	Evangelical
THE BIBLE	24	52	73
RELIGIOUS BOOKS	16	25	34
FELLOW CHRISTIANS	9	24	38
NATURE	27	32	25
RELIGIOUS SERVICES	49	48	57
LISTEN TO SERMONS OR LECTURES	33	42	54
EVANGELISM	6	15	30
MEDITATION	30	36	43
BIBLE GROUP	7	16	26
PRAYER GROUP	16	24	39
RELIGIOUS MAGAZINES	10	16	26
RELIGIOUS TV	14	29	40
SPIRITUAL COUNSELING	6	11	17
COMMUNION	39	30	39
HELPING OTHERS	49	57	60
PRAYER WITH OTHERS FOR SPIRITUAL HEALING	8	18	31
PRAYER ALONE	58	67	76

CHAPTER VII

WHO HAS GREATER NUCLEAR STRENGTH?

	Catholics			Protestants			Total		
	U.S.A.	U.S.S.R.	EVEN	U.S.A.	U.S.S.R.	EVEN	U.S.A.	U.S.S.R.	EVEN
4–5/82	22	35	34	16	44	30	17	40	32
11/82	24	32	32	20	29	36	22	30	33
3/83	18	44	31	13	43	31	15	43	35
2/85	25	19	47	24	23	42	24	23	44

WHICH WILL INCREASE CHANCE OF WAR?

	Catholics		Protestants	
	Arms buildup	U.S.A. fall behind	Arms buildup	U.S.A. fall behind
1983	42	44	34	50
1985	45	42	39	43

CHAPTER VIII

CONSTITUTIONAL AMENDMENT TO BAN ABORTION EXCEPT FOR RAPE, INCEST, AND THREAT TO MOTHER'S LIFE

	Favor	Oppose
EVANGELICALS	66	30
SOUTHERN BAPTISTS	60	38
CATHOLICS	59	38
PROTESTANTS	51	44
METHODISTS	44	53

MORAL DECLINE AS MOST IMPORTANT PROBLEM

	Catholic	Protestant	Total
4/76	2	6	4
4/78	3	4	3

	Catholic	Protestant	Total
1/80	2	2	2
3/80	1	3	2
9/80	1	3	3
1/82	3	4	4
11/83	1	9	6
2/84	4	8	7
6/84	2	6	5
1/85	1	3	2

CHAPTER IX

ERA SUPPORT

	Catholic	Protestant	Total
1975	62	54	58
1976	58	54	57
1980	62	60	58
1981	68	58	63
1982	58	53	56
1984	69	59	63

DEATH PENALTY

	Catholics		Protestants		Total	
	Favor	Oppose	Favor	Oppose	Favor	Oppose
1965	52	38	42	45	45	43
1969	54	37	51	46	51	40
1971	50	42	50	38	44	40
1974	67	33	65	35	64	36

PRESIDENTIAL CANDIDATE BETTER ABLE TO HANDLE ISSUES

	Male better	Female better	Gap	No difference
ECONOMIC CONDITIONS				
CATHOLIC	35	19	+ 16	40
PROTESTANT	45	17	+ 28	30

	Male better	Female better	Gap	No difference
UNEMPLOYMENT				
CATHOLIC	34	20	+ 14	40
PROTESTANT	44	17	+ 27	31
FOREIGN POLICY				
CATHOLIC	54	7	+ 47	33
PROTESTANT	62	9	+ 53	21
SITUATION IN CENTRAL AMERICA				
CATHOLIC	54	8	+ 46	30
PROTESTANT	60	9	+ 51	21
RELATIONS WITH SOVIET UNION				
CATHOLIC	54	12	+ 42	28
PROTESTANT	61	11	+ 50	21
IMPROVING THE QUALITY OF LIFE IN AMERICA				
CATHOLIC	24	37	− 13	35
PROTESTANT	33	31	+ 2	28

CHAPTER X

PARENTS' GRADES FOR SCHOOLS

	Catholics	Protestants	U.S.A.
NATION'S SCHOOLS			
A	3	4	4
B	24	26	24
C	43	41	43
D	11	12	12
F	4	2	3
LOCAL SCHOOLS			
A	7	11	9
B	32	35	33
C	30	30	30
D	13	10	10
F	4	4	4

	Catholics	Protestants	U.S.A.
SCHOOL YOUR OLDEST CHILD ATTENDS			
A	29	28	27
B	47	47	47
C	15	17	17
D	4	4	4
F	2	2	2

SHOULD SCHOOLS HAVE COURSES ON . . .

	Catholics			Protestants		
	Yes	No	Gap	Yes	No	Gap
ALCOHOL ABUSE	84	14	+ 70	77	19	+ 58
DRUG ABUSE	87	11	+ 76	81	16	+ 65
PARENT TRAINING	58	36	+ 22	53	40	+ 13
DANGERS OF NUCLEAR WAR	58	38	+ 20	48	46	+ 2
COMPUTER TRAINING	76	20	+ 56	68	23	+ 45
DRIVER EDUCATION	72	26	+ 46	74	20	+ 54
RACE RELATIONS	58	34	+ 24	55	33	+ 22
COMMUNISM, SOCIALISM	56	38	+ 18	49	38	+ 11
DANGERS OF NUCLEAR WASTE	57	34	+ 23	54	33	+ 21

CHAPTER XI

REAGAN APPROVAL

	Catholics		Protestants	
	Approve	Disapprove	Approve	Disapprove
6/83	46	43	42	42
11/83	53	35	55	36

APPROVAL OF REAGAN'S HANDLING OF ISSUES

	Catholics		Protestants	
	Approve	Disapprove	Approve	Disapprove
OVERALL APPROVAL	66–27		63–29	
ECONOMY	48–43		50–42	

	Catholics		Protestants	
	Approve	*Disapprove*	*Approve*	*Disapprove*
UNEMPLOYMENT	44–45		45–43	
TRADE DEFICIT	39–40		39–40	
BUDGET DEFICIT	37–45		40–44	
TAX REFORM	34–39		39–36	
MIDDLE EAST	43–37		43–34	

PARTY BEST FOR GROUPS

	Catholics		Protestants		Total	
	Rep	*Dem*	*Rep*	*Dem*	*Rep*	*Dem*
BUSINESS/PROFESSIONAL	70	15	68	18	69	16
WHITE COLLAR	56	24	62	22	59	23
SKILLED WORKERS	42	35	42	41	41	39
SMALL BUSINESS	34	46	37	44	35	45
FARMERS	31	47	33	45	31	45
RETIRED	28	50	31	45	28	48
UNEMPLOYED	23	56	30	48	26	52
WOMEN	24	50	29	46	25	48
UNION MEMBERS	23	57	27	57	24	58
UNSKILLED WORKERS	19	60	26	56	22	58
BLACKS	17	65	22	56	19	60
PEOPLE LIKE YOURSELF	44	37	45	37	43	36

INDEX

Abortion
  Catholic views on, 51–52, 93–99, 101–2, 196
  position of the Church on, 91–93, 128
Acquired Immune Deficiency Syndrome (AIDS), 63
AFL-CIO, 75–76
Afterlife, 18–19
Age
  of American Catholics, 3
  and mass attendance, 29
  and religious practice, 32–33, 34
  and satisfaction with the Church, 45, 46
Alcohol consumption, 109–11, 151
Annulment, 45, 50, 182
Arms control
  and nuclear freeze, 83, 181
  peace pastoral on, 31, 77, 82–83
  and SALT II treaty, 83–84
  weapon systems in, 84
Artificial insemination, 100
Atheists, tolerance of, 61, 65

Balanced-budget amendment, 71
Baroni, Geno, 66
Bellagamba, Anthony, 140
Bernardin, Cardinal Joseph, 92
Bible
  illiteracy, 35
  interpretation of, 20–22
  reading, 32, 33, 34–35, 153, 154, 186
  study programs, 176
Birth control
  dissent from the Church on, 6, 50–51, 183
  in sex education, 119
  "Squeal Rule" on, 100–1

Bishops. See Catholic Church
Black Catholics
  and integrated church, 62
  numbers of, 3
Blacks
  parochial school support of, 121
  in South Africa, 89
  tolerant attitude toward, 60, 62–63
B-1 bomber, 84
Brown, Louise, 100
Bryce, Edward, 99
Bush, George, 135, 137

Cambodia, invasion of, 79
Capital punishment, 107–9, 197
Carter, Jimmy, 81, 83, 84, 87, 128, 129, 190
Casino gambling, legalization of, 112
Catholic Church
  on abortion, 91–93, 128
  approval ratings for, 43–50, 181, 183–84
  on Bible, 35
  communal nature of, 22
  dissent from teachings of, 50–52, 178–79, 182–83
  ecumenical activity of, 185
  on Equal Rights Amendment (ERA), 103–4
  expectations for future of, 57
  forms of guidance from, 52
  lay participation in, 44, 49, 53–54, 56–57, 181
  in New Deal coalition, 67
  opportunities for Catholic activity, 184–86
  and public education, 125, 184–85
  on public policy issues, 47–48, 184

202   INDEX

in Central America, 86
opposition to Vietnam War, 82
peace, 66, 77, 82–83, 172, 191
religious revival in, 31, 42, 179
and science, 124
solutions to priest shortage, 53–55
transition to middle-class church, 67–
   68, 183
Catholics
on abortion, 51–52, 93–99, 101–2, 196
affluence of, 68
and alcohol consumption, 109–11, 151
alienated. *See* Unchurched
and anti-Catholicism, 1
attitude to priesthood, 53–56
commitment to peace, 77–78, 90
contribution to society, 188–91
on crime-related issues, 106–9, 197
and education. *See* Education;
   Parochial schools; Public schools
on foreign policy. *See* Foreign policy
   issues
and labor movement, 66–67, 74–76,
   190
on life issues, 99–100
on marijuana use, 111–12, 151
political affiliation of, 126, 131–38, 155,
   156, 180, 190, 200
population growth of, 2
on pornography laws, 113
and presidential politics, 126–31, 190–
   91
profile of, 3–9
"Protestantization" of, 188
and religion. *See* Religious belief;
   Religious practice
and religious broadcasting, 39–42, 75–
   76
on school prayer, 113
support for activist government, 69–74,
   190
tolerant attitudes of, 59–65, 189
visibility of, 2
See also Hispanic Catholics; Men;
   Teenage Catholics; Women
"Catholic Social Teaching and the U.S.
   Economy," 66, 67, 68–69, 72
Catholic University of America, 105
Central America, 85–87
"Challenge of Peace, The," 66, 77, 82–83,
   172
Charismatic Renewal movement, 145
Charity, individual, 8, 38

Church. *See* Catholic Church
Church attendance, 26–29, 51, 153, 179,
   194–95
Clarke, Maura, 85
College-educated Catholics
numbers of, 5
religious practice of, 29, 33–34, 180
satisfaction with the Church, 45, 48
Confession, increase in, 30, 31
Contras, military aid to, 87
Creationism, 21–22
Crime, fear of, 106
Cuomo, Mario, 135, 137

Death penalty, 107–9, 197
Defense spending, 79–82
Deficit reduction, 71
Democratic Party, 47, 126, 131–38, 155,
   156, 200
Devil, beliefs about, 15–16
Diem family, 82
Disarmament. *See* Arms control
Divorce, 6, 45, 50, 158, 170, 176, 182
*Dogmatic Constitution on Divine
   Revelation, The,* 35
Donovan, Jean, 85
Drunk-driving laws, 110

Eagleton, Thomas, 127
Education
Catholic/Protestant consensus on, 116–
   20
Catholic/Protestant differences on,
   120–24
and coed sports, 122
home schools, 121
in nontraditional subjects, 123, 199
religious, 152–53, 166, 172, 174–75
science, 123–24
sex, 119, 150
See also Parochial schools; Public
   schools
Education level
and mass attendance, 29
and religious practice, 33–34
and satisfaction with the Church, 45
See also College-educated Catholics
Eisenhower, Dwight D., 127
Elderly
religious practice of, 34
satisfaction with the Church, 45, 46,
   181–82
El Salvador, 85–86